South Plains College Library

DATE DUE

FEB 2 2 2018			
			PRINTED IN U.S.A.

FIGHTING THE DEATH PENALTY

Eugene G. Wanger, 1986

FIGHTING THE DEATH PENALTY

**A FIFTY-YEAR JOURNEY OF
ARGUMENT AND PERSUASION**

Eugene G. Wanger

MICHIGAN STATE UNIVERSITY PRESS | EAST LANSING

When the conduct of men is designed to be influenced, *persuasion*, kind, unassuming persuasion, should ever be adopted. It is an old and true maxim, that a "drop of honey catches more flies than a gallon of gall." So with men. If you would win a man to your cause, *first* convince him that you are his sincere friend. Therein is a drop of honey that catches his heart, which, say what he will, is the great high road to his reason, and which, when once gained, you will find but little trouble in convincing his judgment of the justice of your cause, if indeed that cause really be a just one.

ABRAHAM LINCOLN, *Springfield, Illinois, February 22, 1842*

Contents

Foreword

Michael L. Radelet

W riting in the 1972 case of *Furman v. Georgia*, which temporarily abolished the death penalty in the United States, Justice Thurgood Marshall asserted that unless citizens supported capital punishment purely on retributive grounds, the more informed they were about the death penalty, the more likely they would be to oppose it. This contention, which has come to be known as "The Marshall Hypothesis," certainly gains credibility when one examines the life's work of Eugene G. Wanger, who is, beyond question, the foremost authority on the history and current status of the death penalty in Michigan. Now, with the publication of this collection of his speeches and essays, students of the death penalty both today and in the future will be able to understand and study his insightful and influential work on the subject.

Few Americans have ever had such a significant and permanent impact on the death penalty than Mr. Wanger (known to friends as "Gil"). In 1846, Michigan became the first western democracy to abolish the death penalty, with the law taking effect on March 1, 1847. Others in the nineteenth century, such as human rights hero Sojourner Truth and renowned jurist Thomas M. Cooley, worked tirelessly to keep it that way. In the pages that follow, readers will learn that as a young lawyer in the early 1960s, Mr. Wanger was elected as one of 144 delegates to attend a convention that would rewrite Michigan's constitution. While the state's electorate was evenly split between Democrats and Republicans, 2/3 of the elected delegates were Republican, most of whom were quite conservative. Mr. Wanger, the youngest Republication delegate, then drafted a proposal to impose a constitutional ban on the death penalty and almost single-handedly steered it through the convention. In the end, there were only three dissenting votes. The new constitution took effect on the first day of 1964, and to this day Michigan remains the only state whose prohibition against executions is written into its constitution.

That victory for death penalty abolitionists has never been sealed in cement. Throughout the past 50 years (although less so more recently) there have been numerous attempts to amend that constitution by putting the ban on the death penalty to a referendum of the voters. A brutal murder combined with adventurous politicians who seek to use the murder for their own political advantage have led to numerous fights over the death penalty since 1963. Always, leading the troops and sitting at the front of the abolitionists' table has been Gil Wanger.

Wanger has used his talents to educate legislators and the public about the top issues in contemporary death penalty debates: whether the death penalty deters more criminal homicides than life imprisonment, the inevitability of executing the innocent, the need to prevent future criminal violence by those already in prison, whether the death penalty can help protect law enforcement officials and prison workers, whether the publicity surrounding the death penalty can actually inspire some to commit murders, and a host of related questions.

Wanger never fought alone. He was able to assemble a formidable group of fellow death penalty opponents, including Professor Art Brandstatter, a former football hero and long-term Head of the School of Criminal Justice at Michigan State, Yale Kamisar, Professor of Law at the University of Michigan, John Hannah, beloved President of Michigan State, Perry Johnson and William Kime from the Michigan Department of Corrections, Dr. LeMoyne Snyder from the Michigan State Police, and scores of others who possessed professional expertise in a given area or who simply raised their voices to stand for "the least among us."

Two points about Wanger's work stand out, at least to me. First, his analyses are data-driven. As such, readers will not find in-depth philosophical, moral, or religious critiques of the death penalty, although such critiques are easily found elsewhere. His is not a "theoretically-based" evaluation of the death penalty. After all, in the final analysis, it matters little what people think about the death penalty "in theory." What matters is what we think about the death penalty *as it is actually applied*—with disparities, racial bias, wrongful convictions, and tremendous economic costs. His work looks at the real world, and how the death penalty operates (or not) in that world. He does not say "I think x, y, and z," he says "The data show a, b, and c." And he is a man who knows the data: his personal library of death penalty books and pamphlets is widely recognized as the most extensive in the world.

Second, too often in death penalty debates we tend to lose respect for our opponents. Of this I personally plead guilty, often finding myself feeling the need for a shower after going head to head with a person whom I believe relies too much on pure hatred to make the pro-death penalty argument. But Gil Wanger is a different breed. To use a boxing analogy, I have seen him go fifteen rounds with a worthy opponent and in the end come out of the ring shaking his opponent's hand. It is a lesson that many of us need to learn.

Thankfully, Gil has lived long enough to see the lessons that he taught Michiganders spread to other parts of the country. In the 1980s, Massachusetts abolished the death penalty, and since 2004 so have New York, New Jersey, New Mexico, Illinois, Connecticut, and Maryland. In 1977, there were 16 abolitionist countries worldwide. By early 2014 there were 97 countries that were totally abolitionist. Eight others have abolished the death penalty for crimes in peacetime, and 35 others are "de facto" abolitionist, with no executions in the past decade. The tally is 140 countries that do not execute and 58 that have still not read Gil Wanger's work.

Hopefully, with the publication of this volume, they will.

Preface

The intense forensic competition of my high school, college and law school years left me with a profound respect for the value of reasoned argument; and the uncommon success which came my way in these endeavors impressed me with the importance of presenting my arguments in the most persuasive way possible.

Since then forty years in the practice of law have brought their wins and losses, as did my political efforts as a Delegate to our state's Constitutional Convention and Chairman of our county's Board of Commissioners; all of which further strengthened my high regard for reason and persuasion.

Warren Buffett, the phenomenally successful investor, when speaking to students at the University of Washington in 1989, said, "How I got here is pretty simple. It's not IQ, I'm sure you'll be glad to hear. The big thing is rationality. I always look at IQ and talent as representing the horsepower of the motor, but that the output—the efficiency with which that motor works—depends on rationality. A lot of people start out with 400-horsepower motors but only get a hundred horsepower of output. It's way better to have a 200-horsepower motor and get it all into output." Moreover, as the philosopher William James observed, "Reason . . . has the unique advantage over its antagonists that its activity never lets up and that it presses always in one direction."[1]

How strongly it presses is shown by who and how many people it convinces. And this is where persuasion comes in. Your arguments must be linked to beliefs, attitudes, values and facts which your audience will accept. And as Lincoln put it, "If you would win a man to your cause, *first* convince him that you are his sincere friend." The more you can do these things, the more people will actually listen to what you have to say.

A calm environment certainly helps. In the words of Justice Brandeis, "To the exercise of good judgment calmness is, in times of deep feeling and on subjects which excite passion, as essential as fearlessness and honesty."

Calmness, however, was frequently absent from my environment, when as Co-Chairman of the Michigan Committee Against Capital Punishment with my old friend and fellow Co-Chair, Tom Downs, I was called upon over the years to help stem the tide of opinion favoring the death penalty. The situation was made more contentious by the facts that my state was the first government in the English-speaking world to abolish that penalty for murder and lesser crimes, had never restored it and now had a constitution which banned it; and that consequently some politicians seemed to think it would be a great feather in their cap, and gain them a great deal of publicity, if they could bring the death penalty back.

The 40 items contained in this volume demonstrate how I coped. They are set out in chronological order from 1962 to 2015 and show my attempt to inform and persuade the public and its opinion leaders about the evils of capital punishment and why they should reject it. It has been an exciting adventure. All were written (or spoken) by me and all their venues are Michigan, except as otherwise stated in the table of contents. The circular design on the front cover is the logotype of the Committee.

Before this work went to press, Arthur Sulzberger, Jr., through his spokeswoman, objected to the inclusion of three articles from his paper, *The New York Times*, unless a fee of $1,140.00 was paid in return for a license so restrictive that to include the articles would impair the ability of the publisher to market the book. Unwilling to countenance the fee or the restrictions, but mindful of the significance of the articles to the death penalty debate in which I was engaged, I have abstracted them for the reader.

My very special thanks are due to Professor Michael Radelet of the University of Colorado at Boulder, and a most distinguished death penalty scholar, for writing the Foreword; to Rev. Dr. Lloyd Hall for permission to include his testimony, which was important to the campaign and is the finest brief statement of the Christian position on the death penalty that I have ever seen; and to the staff of the Michigan State University Press, especially to Ms. Julie Loehr, Editor-in-Chief, and to Ms. Kristine Blakeslee, Managing Editor, for their extraordinary patience and skillful work with this unusually complicated manuscript.

It remains for me to express my undying gratitude to my wife, Marilyn, for her wonderful support and assistance in these endeavors, and to the many friends who have helped me along the way.

E.G.W.
Lansing, Michigan
September 2, 2016

NOTE

1. The remarks of Warren Buffett are quoted from Carol J. Loomis's fine book, *Tap Dancing to Work* (New York: Penguin Group, 2012), 134.

FIGHTING THE
DEATH PENALTY

1.

Date: ___1-11-62___

Mr. ___Hoxie___ submitted the following:

The Committee on ___Legislative Powers___ reports:

Committee Proposal No. ___20.___

1   A proposal to provide that no law shall be enacted providing

2 for the penalty of death.

3   (Amends Article V by adding a new section.)

4

5   THE COMMITTEE RECOMMENDS THAT THE FOLLOWING
           BE INCLUDED IN THE CONSTITUTION:

6

7   Sec. A. NO LAW SHALL BE ENACTED PROVIDING FOR THE PENALTY

8 OF DEATH.

9

10

11

12

13

14

15

16   Chairman.

17

18

19

20

21

22

With the recommendation that it pass.

The proposal was referred to the Committee of the Whole and placed on General Orders.

2.

CONSTITUTIONAL CONVENTION OF MICHIGAN

Date___1-11-62_____

Mr. Hoxie, Chairman of the Committee on Legislative Powers, submitted the following reasons in support of Committee Proposal No.___20___:

Michigan in 1846 was the first American State and the first governmental jurisdiction in the English-speaking world to legislate against capital punishment. Except for treason, which today is clearly more a matter of federal rather than state significance, our state has not had the death penalty since that time.

The compelling arguments against capital punishment were succinctly re-stated in the Journal of the American Judicature Society of October, 1958, as follows:

1. The evidence clearly shows that execution does not act as a deterrent to capital crimes.

2. The serious offenses are committed, except in rare instances, by those suffering from mental disturbances; are impulsive in nature; and are not the acts of the "criminal" class.

3. Conviction of the innocent does occur and death makes a miscarriage of justice irrevocable. Human judgment cannot be infallible.

4. When the death sentence is removed as a possible punishment, more convictions are possible with less delays.

5. Unequal application of the law takes place because those executed are often the poor, the ignorant, and the unfortunate without resources.

6. The State sets a bad example when it takes a life. Imitative crimes and murder are stimulated by executions.

7. Legally taking a life is useless and demoralizing to the general public. It is also demoralizing to the public officials who, dedicated to rehabilitating individuals, must callously put a man to death. The effect upon fellow prisoners can be imagined.

8. A trial where a life may be at stake is highly sensationalized, adversely affects the administration of justice, and is bad for the community.

9. Society is amply protected by a sentence of life imprisonment.

Since 1926 there have been 8 times that a majority of one of the houses of our legislature voted in favor of the death penalty. Thus there is potential danger, particularly after a sensational crime, of such legislation being adopted.

The Committee believes that it is both fitting and opportune for Michigan to step forward in the tradition which we began over 115 years ago and that the adoption of this provision

2

Reasons
Committee Proposal No. 20

would be a significant contribution to the concept of civilized justice which all of us seek to serve.

T. Jefferson Hope,
Chairman.

3. Verbatim Debate of the Michigan Constitutional Convention on Committee Proposal 20, on January 16 & April 30, 1962, from its OFFICIAL RECORD, 595–598, 2968

IN THE COMMITTEE OF THE WHOLE—
FIFTY-EIGHTH DAY, TUESDAY

January 6, 1962

CHAIRMAN HUTCHINSON: The Chair recognizes the chairman of the [Legislative Powers] committee, Mr. Hoxie.

MR. HOXIE: Mr. Chairman and fellow delegates, this, to me, is one of the most serious proposals that we will have before this committee. It is not only clear but it is concise. There cannot be any misunderstanding as to its intent and purpose.

To me it is twofold. The question that you have got to settle in your minds is: do you think it is right for the state to take a human life? The other is: do you feel that this is an undue restriction upon the legislature?

Our committee considered this. We have secured a lot of data on it, both the arguments pro and con, and at this time I would yield to Mr. Millard, who will furnish that information to the delegates.

CHAIRMAN HUTCHINSON: The Chair recognizes Mr. Millard.

MR. MILLARD: Mr. Chairman, members of the committee, this is a proposed new section to the proposed new constitution, but it is not a new concept in the jurisprudence of this state. In 1848 the first statue was passed prohibiting execution of the death penalty in the state of Michigan. There are a great many reasons why the committee voted to put out this proposal, and one was for the many times that this question arises and is proposed as a legislative matter to our state legislators.

I might say that in my own personal experience over a great many years as a practicing lawyer, each time a heinous and atrocious crime was committed in the state of Michigan there were some people who immediately advocated the death penalty, even though it wouldn't be retroactive and take charge of that particular case. And so many, many, many times there have been bills presented to the legislature to provide for the death penalty.

When I was attorney general there was a bill introduced every single year, and I think we will have that discussed by one of the other members of the committee to give you just an idea as to how far back these legislative proposals have gone. However, I heard a great many of the arguments both for and against capital punishment in those days, and as you probably all know the elective officials in those days would go around to "government days" held in high schools all over the state, and generally one of the questions that was asked was: "What do you think of capital punishment?" and it fell upon me to make the answers. So I had to look up some of the statistics, some of the things that prompted me to come to the conclusion that capital punishment is not the solution to crime.

In fact, all of these statistics show that crime is greater in a percentage factor according to population in states that do have capital punishment than those that do not.

I want to read here some of the compelling arguments which have been compiled and restated in the Journal of the American Judicature Society of 1958 as follows:

1. The evidence clearly shows that execution does not act as a deterrent to capital crimes.
2. The serious offenses are committed, except in rare instances, by those suffering from mental disturbances; are impulsive in nature; and are not the acts of the "criminal" class.

I believe if all of you will think back to some of the worst crimes you know, you will find that the statement will be verified in your own experience.

3. Conviction of the innocent does occur and death makes a miscarriage of justice irrevocable. Human judgment cannot be infallible.
4. When the death sentence is removed as a possible punishment, more convictions are possible with less delay.
5. Unequal application of the law takes place because those executed are often the poor, the ignorant, and the unfortunate without resources.

That will be enlarged upon by one of the other members of the committee. It is very, very important as far as the humanitarian aspect is concerned.

6. The state sets a bad example when it takes a life.
7. Legally taking a life is useless and demoralizing to the general public. It is also demoralizing to the public officials who, dedicated to rehabilitating individuals, must callously put a man to death. The effect upon fellow prisoners can be imagined.
8. A trial where a life may be at stake is highly sensationalized, adversely affects the administration of justice and is bad for the community.

And, finally,

9. Society is amply protected by a sentence of life imprisonment.

Those are the general reasons, and I would like to have the privilege of calling upon my committee, if the chairman will so let me yield the floor to the members of my subcommittee, and the first I would like to call upon Mr. Wanger.

CHAIRMAN HUTCHINSON: Mr. Millard yields to Mr. Wanger.

MR. WANGER: Thank you, Mr. Millard. Mr. Chairman, members of the committee, this recommendation carries the unanimous vote of the committee on legislative powers, and its report stating these reasons, as you know, appears in the journal on page 305.

The committee believes that it is both fitting and opportune for Michigan to step forward in the tradition which she began, as Mr. Millard pointed out, over 115 years ago; and that the adoption of this provision would be a significant contribution to the concept of civilized justice which all of us seek to serve.

The arguments have been very well stated in the committee's report, but I would like to enlarge particularly upon the fourth one, which, as pointed out, is that when the death sentence is removed as a possible punishment, more convictions are possible with less delay.

I received a letter on December 15 from Dr. LeMoyne Snyder, a former resident of the Lansing area, and a nationally recognized authority in the field of legal medicine. He writes as follows from California, where he now resides:

> Within the last week I have returned from a murder trial in Oklahoma, and during the past 39 years I have been involved in murder trials in a great many different states—most of them with capital punishment.
>
> One fact that few people realize is the ease and speed with which a murder trial is conducted in Michigan or other states which do not have capital punishment. In fact, a sizeable proportion of the cases in noncapital punishment states require no trial at all because you have a plea of guilty to start with, which rarely happens where capital punishment is involved.
>
> Here in California at the present time there are 35 inmates of death row awaiting execution. Some of them have been there for years and within the past year one person was executed after 12 years. In fact it isn't far from

the truth that Chessman served both a life sentence and a death sentence but, whether he was guilty or not, the fact remains that his conviction and execution required an enormous amount of time, trouble and expense.

You may know that in this state, as well as in several others, the jury makes 2 entirely separate determinations—first a finding of whether the defendant is guilty or not. If the jury finds him guilty, they then listen to several days of testimony as to whether the death sentence should be inflicted. It happens quite often that the jury will find him guilty and then disagree on the punishment. This requires that a new jury be empaneled just to determine the punishment and it requires retrying the entire case over again.

One of the greatest benefits of not having capital punishment is the fact that the ends of justice is much better served.

CHAIRMAN HUTCHINSON: Mr. Millard.

MR. MILLARD: Mr. Chairman, I would like now to call upon Mr. Downs, who will take it from the legislative angle.

MR. DOWNS: Mr. Millard, Mr. Chairman, delegates to the convention, I rise to speak in favor of the committee proposal which has, as was mentioned, a unanimous recommendation.

As was pointed out by other speakers, Michigan has a proud history in being the first state by law to eliminate capital punishment. However, from the year 1903 through 1956 there were 25 bills and resolutions dealing with capital punishment. In 8 cases proposals for capital punishment passed at least one house. In 1929 it passed both houses, to be vetoed by Governor Green. In 1931 the capital punishment provision passed both houses, was signed by the governor, with the proviso for a referendum, and the people defeated this by a vote of 352,000 to 269,000. So capital punishment did not become the law.

I think perhaps that Mr. Wanger has summarized the position of the committee best when he says that this recommendation is another step forward in civilized justice; a step that Michigan can historically be proud of, and I hope this committee will support the report of our committee.

CHAIRMAN HUTCHINSON: Mr. Millard.

MR. MILLARD: Mr. Chairman, I would like to call upon the next member of my subcommittee, Mrs. Koeze.

MRS. KOEZE: Ladies and gentlemen, I would just like to have you refer to journal, page 306, argument 5 of the committee report.

Warden Lewis E. Lawes, of Sing Sing prison, a most eminent authority who knows first hand whereof he speaks, said of the 150 offenders that he was required to escort to the death chamber:

> In one respect they were all alike. All were poor and most of them friendless. Juries do not intentionally favor the rich—the law is theoretically impartial—but the defendant with ample means is able to have his case presented with every favorable aspect, while the poor defendant often has a lawyer assigned by the courts. Usually the lawyer assigned has had no experience in a capital case.
>
> Thus it is seldom that it happens that a person who is able to have eminent defense attorneys is convicted of murder in the first degree, and very rare indeed that such a person is executed.

Ladies and gentlemen, I think this points up very, very thoroughly what we have facing us here, and I do hope that this committee will give serious consideration to this section that we in the legislative powers committee deemed absolutely necessary to put in the Michigan constitution. Thank you.

MR. MILLARD: Mr. Chairman, just a final word. As has been stated, the legislative powers committee was unanimous in this recommendation that this proposal be adopted. I think it has been pointed out very clearly that capital punishment does not deter crime. Furthermore, there have been instances of innocent men being convicted, and if one is put to death there can be no appeal from that sentence.

I hope that the committee will adopt this proposal. Mr. Millard yields the floor.

CHAIRMAN HUTCHINSON: Mr. Bentley.

MR. BENTELY: Mr. Chairman, at the outset I would like to say I am sympathetic to the committee's proposal, but there are certain portions of the committee report which tend to disturb me. I wonder if Mr. Millard would indicate whether or not the adoption of this report might be taken as criticism by this convention of any jurisdiction which does inflict capital punishment for any reason whatsoever?

MR. MILLARD: Nowhere have we indicated that any other jurisdiction should be criticized. We made the general statement that capital punishment has not proven a deterrent in crime in other states, and the statistics will bear that out. We are not criticizing; we are just citing facts.

MR. BENTLEY: I wonder if Mr. Millard, then, would indicate as to whether or not the committee might feel that the federal government errs in taking lives in cases of, for example, espionage and similar situations where the death penalty is invoked.

MR. MILLARD: A crime against the patriotism of the country, and a crime against our country, should be punished by death. But we don't have that in this state. The federal government has preempted treason, and I am all for the death penalty as far as treason and espionage, and anything that has to do with the welfare and safety of our country.

MR. BENTLEY: Then, in other words, Mr. Chairman, the reasons adduced here by the subcommittee for taking a position against capital punishment would certainly not apply, in their opinion, to crime against the state or the nation, whether in this country or any other country.

MR. MILLARD: Certainly not. Not against our country, no. sir.

MR. BENTLEY: Thank you.

CHAIRMAN HUTCHINSON: Are there any amendments to the body of the proposal? Mr. Martin.

MR. MARTIN: I just want to comment on this proposal, because I served in the legislature when one or more of these proposals to adopt capital punishment in the state of Michigan came before us. They always come when there has been a particularly serious crime and when emotion is at its highest. I think it is significant that after the legislation has been considered and the people have cooled a little bit, particularly in the case where it was submitted to the people, the people have turned it down.

I also had the privilege of serving for some years as chairman of the Michigan Crime and Delinquency Council, which is an arm of the National Council on Crime and Delinquency, and the opinion of that body, and of the many experts who serve it, including many judges who work with the council, is, I think, uniform that the arguments advanced by the committee are sound and that the death penalty is not a deterrent to crime.

It seems to me I remember also from studies we saw that in England, when the death penalty was given for matters as small as stealing a loaf of bread—in fact, it was used on all kinds of situations—crime was never higher. This is in the earlier history of England, so it seems quite clear it doesn't act as a deterrent and that it is only an act of vengeance on the part of the public.

It seems to me that this is a splendid proposal; that it is completely sound, and particularly sound because it is being considered at a time when we don't happen to be subject to some of the high emotion that affects this question from time to time. I think it is a good time for the people of Michigan to settle once and for all the question of capital punishment.

CHAIRMAN HUTCHINSON: Mr. Norris.

MR. NORRIS: Mr. Chairman, I rise also to support the committee, and I just want to make one statement. I support the right of every person in Michigan not to be put to death under the death penalty. I think that is a right which is stated here conversely in the proscription against a law in this field.

CHAIRMAN HUTCHINSON: Mr. Cudlip.

MR. CUDLIP: Mr. Chairman, I would like to ask Mr. Millard a question just so I can clear my mind. Am I correct in assuming that by statute today treason in Michigan is punishable by death?

MR. MILLARD: I don't know whether I can answer that.

MR. CUDLIP: Well, I recall a few years ago, that there was a bank robbery, and I believe it was in Midland, and in connection with that there were some killings and, of course, the federal government took charge, and the convicted were hung at Milan because the federal law said the punishment should be that highest punishment afforded by the law of the state in which the crime occurred.

I am in favor of this proposal, but I have heard talk here about Michigan's leadership, and last night we adopted a proposal which said that in connection with commutations, reprieves and so forth, treason would be dealt with as other crimes. That is not too germane, but it is somewhat germane, but, if my memory serves me, treason against Michigan is now punishable by death, and I suppose if we adopt this, that would go off the books, and that is all right with me. But I think that is an interesting point, and I just wondered what the answer was.

CHAIRMAN HUTCHINSON: Mr. Danhof.

MR. DANHOF: Mr. Chairman, to answer Mr. Cudlip, I think the federal government has made provision in this regard that where it calls for the death penalty, as in the case that he speaks of—a murder took place in a federally insured bank—there may be executed a death penalty, and it provides that the execution shall be carried out by the U.S. marshal in the same manner as provided by the state laws; except that there is no such provision in the state law, it shall be as the court shall prescribe.

If what you are concerned with is the fact that we might be infringing—have to have a federal amendment—this is not necessarily the case. It merely is that if it is found that the death penalty in the state law provides for execution by the electric chair, that will be used; or by hanging, or in some states they even have firing squads yet. But it provides also that in cases there is no death penalty, then the court shall prescribe, and I think the method prescribed—if it is not in the statute—is by hanging.

There is no connection any more between the two.

CHAIRMAN HUTCHINSON: Mr. Wanger.

MR. WANGER: In reply also to your question, Mr. Cudlip, treason is punishable by death under Michigan Statutes Annotated 28.812. Also the case of '37, the Chebatoris case was tried under the national bank robbery act. It was the first case there tried, and it was done entirely pursuant to federal law as far as the conviction was concerned. I would merely add that if a situation should arise where Michigan's prohibition of the death penalty, as is here proposed, should make it inconvenient or impossible to execute a federally imposed sentence of death within the confines of the state of Michigan, that would be no great loss.

MR. CUDLIP: Mr. Chairman, was Mr. Wanger's answer that Michigan does now presently punish treason with death?

MR. WANGER: By statute.

MR. CUDLIP: Thank you. This is the information I wanted. I am in favor of the proposal.

CHAIRMAN HUTCHINSON: Are there any amendments to the body of the proposal? If not, it will pass

Committee Proposal 20 is passed.

·　　·　　·

IN THE CONVENTION

April 30, 1962

SECRETARY CHASE: Item 30 on the calendar, Committee Proposal 20. A proposal to provide that no law shall be enacted providing for the penalty of death. Amends article V by adding a new section.

PRESIDENT NISBET: Mr. Hoxie.

MR. HOXIE: Mr. President, fellow delegates, the committee on style and drafting again couldn't find any change to make in the proposal as it was adopted by the convention. It is short, clear, concise and, I think, understandable to every delegate here.

PRESIDENT NISBET: Mr. Baginski.

MR. BAGINSKI: Mr. President and fellow delegates, we have no objections to Wanger's "no kill 'em" proposal.

PRESIDENT NISBET: Will the delegates please clear the board? Those in favor of Committee Proposal 20 will vote aye. Those opposed will vote nay. Have you all voted? If so, the secretary will lock the machine and record the vote.
  The roll was called and the delegates voted as follows:

YEAS—108

Allen	Gust	Plank
Andrus, Miss	Habermehl	Pollock
Anspach	Hart, Miss	Powell
Austin	Haskill	Prettie
Baginski	Hatch	Pugsley
Balcer	Hatcher, Mrs.	Radka
Barthwell	Heideman	Rajkovich
Batchelor	Higgs	Richards, J.B.

Beaman	Hodges	Richards, L.W.
Bentley	Hood	Romney
Binkowski	Howes	Rood
Blandford	Hoxie	Sablich
Brake	Hubbs	Seyferth
Brown, G.E.	Hutchinson	Shackleton
Buback	Jones	Shaffer
Butler, Mrs.	Karn	Sharpe
Cudlip	Kelsey	Sleder
Cushman, Mrs.	King	Spitler
Danhof	Kirk, S.	Stafseth
DeVries	Knirk, B.	Staiger
Donnelly, Miss	Koeze, Mrs.	Stamm
Douglas	Krolikowski	Stopczynski
Downs	Kuhn	Suzore
Elliott, A.G.	Lawrence	Tubbs
Elliott, Mrs. Daisy	Leibrand	Turner
Erickson	Leppien	Tweedie
Everett	Lesinski	Upton
Farnsworth	Martin	Van Dusen
Faxon	McAllister	Walker
Figy	McCauley	Wanger
Finch	McGowan, Miss	White
Follo	Millard	Wilkowski
Ford	Murphy	Wood
Gadola	Norris	Woolfenden
Goebel	Ostrow	Yeager
Gover	Page	Young

■   ■   ■

NAYS—3

Doty, Dean	Stevens	Thomason

—

SECRETARY CHASE: On the passage of Committee Proposal 20, the yeas are 108; the nays, 3.

PRESIDENT NISBET: Committee Proposal 20 is passed and referred to committee on style and drafting.

4. House Committee on Constitutional Revision and Women's Rights: Testimony of Eugene G. Wanger, Co-Chairman of the Michigan Committee against Capital Punishment, in Opposition to Michigan House Joint Resolution "B"

March 15, 1973.

Michigan, by statute in 1846, was the first governmental jurisdiction in the English-speaking world to abolish capital punishment for murder and lesser crimes. Our state has never restored it.

If House Joint Resolution "B" is adopted by the legislature, the resulting capital punishment campaign will consume an immense amount of time, attention, effort and money which could otherwise be used to effectively fight and prevent crime. It will successfully divert public attention from effective ways of strengthening Michigan's criminal law and law enforcement system. Considering the seriousness of the crime problem, this would be a tragedy.

Clearly the proponents of the Resolution must bear the burden of proving why Michigan should enact a law which empowers the state to take human life, and in general to threaten the public with that taking of life, in a state which has not had such a law for 127 years.

Not only is the death penalty useless in fighting or preventing crime, it is immensely harmful to society. Even leaving aside the cruelty and terror it inflicts on the condemned and his or her innocent family, the evidence shows:

1. Conviction of the innocent does sometimes occur, and execution makes a miscarriage of justice irrevocable.
2. Capital punishment causes murders and imitative crimes.
3. The death penalty discriminates against the poor, ignorant, friendless and members of minority groups; not only because they are most often convicted, but because of all persons convicted they are the ones more often executed.
4. The death penalty costs the taxpayers a great deal more than life imprisonment.
5. Capital punishment adversely affects the administration of justice.

Let us examine the above reasons one at a time.

1. In Michigan since 1910, at least 8 persons have been wrongfully convicted of murder. Later, for most of them years later, they were proved innocent and freed. They are Robert MacGregor, Alexander Ripan, Lloyd Prevost, Vance Hardy, Gerald Crowden, Louis Gross, "Paget" and Willie Calloway. How many of these innocent men would have been executed if Michigan had had the death penalty? Thomas Jefferson said, "I shall ask for the abolition of the punishment of death until I have the infallibility of human judgment presented to me." Has Michigan demonstrated that infallibility?
2. Capital punishment causes murder as an invitation to the mentally disturbed, through the sensational publicity which always surrounds it, and by the moral lesson it teaches. There are numbers of documented cases where disturbed persons used capital punishment as a means of suicide; afraid to take their own life, they murdered so that the state would do it for them. Similarly, other persons have been directly stimulated to commit murder and imitative crimes by the unrestrained sensational publicity which is present wherever capital punishment

is involved in a trial. No one knows how much murder is indirectly caused by the moral lesson capital punishment teaches, which is that killing is a permissible—even desirable—solution to human problems.

3. Although many persons are dedicated to bringing unjust discrimination to an end, the fact is that capital punishment is discriminatorily applied against the poor, the ignorant, the friendless and members of minority groups; not only because they are most often convicted of capital crimes, but because of all persons convicted of those crimes they are the ones more often executed. The rate of execution of blacks in America far exceeds the proportion of capital crimes committed by black defendants. Even leaving out the southern states, look at the evidence for the North. As reported by the Washington Research Project in 1971,

A study of commutations in Pennsylvania between 1914 and 1958 revealed that whites were nearly twice as likely as blacks to have their sentence commuted. A similar study in New Jersey found almost precisely the same pattern—whites were twice as likely as blacks to have death sentences commuted. In Ohio, over a ten-year period, 78 per cent of blacks sentenced to death were actually executed, while only 51 per cent of whites were.

4. Capital punishment costs the taxpayers substantially more than life imprisonment because the cost saved by killing a prisoner is greatly exceeded by the increased litigation and prison expenses of death penalty cases. The trial is generally much longer and is fully fought out at every point—from selecting the jury to the last desperate appeal—when the defendant's life may be at stake. The Sirhan and Manson murder trials alone are said to have cost the state of California close to a million dollars. On the prison side alone, Richard McGee, administrator of the California correctional system, has written:

The actual costs of execution, the cost of operating the super-maximum security condemned unit, the years spent by some inmates in condemned status, and a pro-rata share of top level prison officials' time spent in administering the unit add up to a cost substantially greater than the cost to retain them in prison the rest of their lives.

5. The death penalty adversely affects the administration of justice at the trial and appellate levels. Experience shows that juries often refuse to convict when death may result. Moreover, as U.S. Attorney General Robert H. Jackson put it, "When the penalty is death appellate judges are tempted to strain the evidence, and in close cases the law, in order to give doubtfully condemned men another chance." James V. Bennett, former director of the Federal Bureau of Prisons, testified before congress a few years ago:

At bottom, the retention of the death penalty has led to all sorts of controversial not to say inconsistent and erratic decisions of our courts on such things as mental responsibility for crime, use of confessions, admissibility of evidence, arrest and arraignment procedures and so on. We might not have the *Miranda, Escobedo, Mallory, Durham*, and other decisions were it not for the fact that the death penalty was involved.

5. Does the Parole Risk of Convicted Murderers Justify Reviving the Death Penalty in Michigan?

Surprising as it may seem to advocates of the death penalty, paroled murderers are clearly the best risks of any class of offenders. Not only in Michigan, but nationally.

As Perry Johnson, Director of the Michigan Department of Corrections, pointed out in February, 1974, of all convicted first degree murderers paroled in Michigan since the state's parole board was established in 1938, not one has been returned to prison for committing another murder. Of the 395 who were paroled since 1938, only 10 were returned for any reason and 5 of those were for technical parole violations.

A study at the Department by Assistant Professor Jack Schwartz of Lansing Community College reveals that the first degree murderers paroled in Michigan between 1959 and 1972 had served an average sentence of 25 years each before release. In Michigan no one convicted of first degree murder can ever be paroled unless their sentence is commuted by the Governor.

Parole data available from 7 other states were summarized four years ago by the Friends Committee on Legislation in *This Life We Take*, as follows:

	PAROLED MURDERERS	SECOND IMPRISONMENT FOR MURDER
California (1945–54)	342	1
Connecticut (1947–60)	60	0
Maryland (1936–61)	37	0
Massachusetts (1900–58)	10	0
Ohio (1945–60)	169	0
New York (1950–59)	357	1
Rhode Island (1915–58)	19	0

Similarly, the national *Uniform Parole Reports Newsletter* of December, 1972, shows that of the 6,908 persons paroled after conviction for Willful Homicide during the years 1965–1969, 98.23% were successful on parole during the crucial first year after release. They had no new major convictions or allegations of offenses resulting in their return to prison. "Willful Homicide" in this study included all degrees of murder and all types of manslaughter except negligent manslaughter, manslaughter by vehicle, or negligent homicide.

Courtesy of Michigan Committee Against Capital Punishment

1202 Mich. National Tower, Lansing 48933

6. Death—Ultimate Penalty—Proves Itself the Ultimate Injustice for All

Eugene G. Wanger

Michigan, by statute in 1846, was the first government in the English-speaking world to abolish capital punishment for murder and lesser crimes. Our state has never restored it. A drive is now being made to amend Michigan's Constitution to directly impose a mandatory death penalty for all first-degree murder and to open the door for that penalty to be applied to other crimes as well. Clearly the proponents must bear the burden of proving why we should enact a rule of law requiring our government to take human life, and in general to threaten the public with that taking of life, in a state which has been without such a law for 128 years.

The barbarity of killing by the state is highlighted by the fact that it is both useless in preventing crime and harmful to society: It fails to deter murder. It causes the death of innocent persons by occasionally executing the innocent and by inciting additional murders by the mentally disturbed. It makes it harder to fight crime because juries often refuse to convict the guilty when the defendant's life is at stake. It is inflicted discriminatorily against blacks, even in northern states, making the ultimate penalty the ultimate injustice.

Deterrence means fewer murders. If the death penalty deterred murder more than life imprisonment it would show up in the homicide rate, for with rare exceptions all homicides in America since the 1920s have been reported. Specifically, if it deterred, there would be a lower homicide rate in states having the death penalty, the rate would go up when the penalty is abolished and go down when it is restored, and in those localities where it is carried out there would be fewer killings near the time of well publicized executions when any deterrent effect would be greatest.

However, 40 years of studies (and probably no subject in criminology has been studied more) demonstrate that none of these things happen. What they show is that there is no correlation between the ups and downs of homicide and the presence or absence of the death penalty. It's like an automobile. If your car runs at exactly the same speed regardless of whether its brakes are on or off, that's pretty strong evidence that the brakes are not working. The logical implication is clear: If would-be murderers think of the consequences at all, they are either deterred by the prospect of life imprisonment as much as they are by the death penalty or they are planning on not getting caught.

Conviction of the innocent does occur, and execution makes a miscarriage of justice irrevocable. In Michigan alone since 1910, at least nine persons are known to have been wrongly convicted of murder. Later, for most of them years later, they were proved innocent and freed. They are Robert MacGregor, Alexander Ripan, Lloyd Prevost, Vance Hardy, Gerald Crowden, Louis Gross, "Paget," Willie Calloway and Charles Clark. How many other innocent men and women have been convicted of murder "beyond a reasonable doubt" by perjured testimony, mistaken identification, or even (as evidence was produced to show in the case of Louis Gross) a "frame-up"? Considering how hard it is to uncover the facts after conviction, let alone after execution, it is obvious that there are more of these miscarriages of justice than we know. Thomas Jefferson said, "I shall ask for the abolition of the punishment of death until I have the infallibility of human judgment presented to me." Has Michigan demonstrated that infallibility?

Capital punishment causes additional murders. These include the so-called "suicide-murder" cases, many of them clinically documented of persons who wanted but feared to take their own lives and committed murder so that the state would execute them. They include imitative killings by the weak-minded, who are incited by the sensational publicity of capital trials. A famous example is the Michigan murder by Alfred Hotelling in the wake of the California Hickman trial in the '20s. No one knows how many murders are indirectly caused by the moral lesson which the death penalty teaches to many: That killing is a permissible, even desirable solution to human problems. As Professor Morris and Hawkins said in their book, *The Honest Politician's Guide to Crime Control,* "If . . . we are to be sincere in our efforts to reduce violence, there is one type of violence that we can with complete certainty eliminate. That is the killing of criminals by the state. The question is, Will people learn to respect life better by threat or by example? And the uniform answer of history, comparative studies, and experience is that man is an emulative animal . . ." As Bernard Shaw put it, "Murder and capital punishment are not opposites that cancel one another, but similars that breed their kind."

The death penalty also makes it harder to fight crime in a number of ways, particularly by obstructing that certainty and swiftness of conviction and punishment which is society's best deterrent to crime. Experience shows that juries often refuse to convict when the penalty is death; and that where the penalty is life imprisonment, more convictions are possible with less delays. It is far better that two murderers go to prison, than that one be executed and the other go free.

Revival of the death penalty will severely aggravate racial tension because it has been inflicted disproportionately against the poor, and especially the black. Of all persons executed in America since 1930, 53.3 per cent have been black though blacks have made up only about 10% of the population. As the Washington Research Project pointed out in The Case Against Capital Punishment, the pattern is particularly evident after sentencing: Even studies in Pennsylvania and New Jersey revealed that whites were twice as likely as blacks to have their death sentences commuted; and in Ohio, over a 10-year period, 78 per cent of blacks sentenced to death were executed, while only

51 percent of whites were. Despite Michigan's progress toward racial justice, it is wishful thinking to assert that, "It can't happen here."

Finally, society is amply protected by life imprisonment. As Perry Johnson, director of the Michigan Dept. of Corrections, recently pointed out, of all convicted first-degree murderers paroled in Michigan since the state's parole board was established in 1938, not one has been returned to prison for committing another murder. Of the 395 who were paroled since 1938, only 10 were returned for any reason and five of those were for technical parole violations.

EUGENE G. WANGER is co-chairman of the Michigan Committee Against Capital Punishment and authored the prohibition of the death penalty included in the 1963 Michigan Constitution.

Michigan State News (East Lansing), April 30, 1974.

7. Testimony of Eugene G. Wanger before the Capital Punishment Task Force of the Michigan Advisory Commission on Criminal Justice, February 10, 1975, Holt, Michigan

Mr. McConnell, Ladies and Gentlemen:

There's been some discussion about the death penalty and I must say that last Wednesday when Glen Bachelder of your staff called me and explained about this hearing this afternoon, I immediately began to consider what I ought to say: because, contrary to what Kirby[1] unintentionally implied, we don't have an "act" that we present. He doesn't give a set speech every time. I certainly don't. And I might say, speaking for our group, that we're constantly receiving factual information and analysis from all over the United States upon this issue, and we're getting a lot more information than anyone ever had before from Michigan. So, as I was thinking about this Wednesday, I turned on the TV as I usually do to get the 11 o'clock news and, on either CBS or NBC, they reported that a small Colorado town, I forget the name now, had just adopted an Animal Control Ordinance which, as written, provided that "if any pet picked up by the Dog Warden is not claimed within 48 hours the owner will be destroyed." Well, I thought that was especially unfortunate in my frame of mind as I was trying to come up, as I'm glad to do today, with an informal but organized talk with you upon the subject that you've decided to consider as a Task Force: the possible restoration of the death penalty.

For those of you I don't know personally, my name is Eugene G. Wanger. I'm co-chairman with Tom Downs of the Michigan Committee Against Capital Punishment. Mr. Downs sends his regrets that he could not on such short notice re-arrange his professional commitments to be present today. We're both lawyers, who two years ago, organized this voluntary citizens' group to oppose the death penalty and to help inform an appallingly uninformed public of the evidence which clearly shows both the futility and the danger of capital punishment. We have attracted very little financial but much responsible moral support, and our executive committee includes Arthur Brandstatter, head of the School of Criminal Justice at Michigan State, D. Hale Brake, long-time well known public servant in Michigan, Perry Johnson, head of the state Department of Corrections, Bill Cahalan, Wayne County Prosecutor, Professor Yale Kamisar of Michigan, Professor George of Wayne, John A. Hannah, and a number of other persons who I'm sure you will recognize as being very thoughtful and very concerned, dedicated persons to the public welfare of our State and our Country.

Day before yesterday I received this form-letter from one of your offices which stated that the members of your commission were studying capital punishment among other issues "in an attempt to come up with recommendations for action." Like that Colorado Ordinance, I think those words, at least as respecting the death penalty, are singularly ill-chosen and I hope inadvertently chosen: For our State, by statute in 1846, was the first governmental jurisdiction in the English-speaking world to abolish the death penalty for murder and lesser crimes and has never restored it. We believe that you as a Task Force and as members of the Michigan Criminal Justice Commission have not only a unique opportunity but, frankly, indeed a signal responsibility to strongly recommend that no action be taken to restore the death penalty for any crime, and especially to inform the public of the cogent and compelling reasons why. So long as the public is agitated by this sensational issue then just so long will both public and official attention be diverted from finding and pursuing effective ways to fight and prevent crime.

I will not dwell at all upon the constitutional or the religious aspects of the question, unless you want to ask me about it perhaps later on, although those aspects are important. Neither will I dwell specifically on the injustice of the death penalty except to emphasize this: That unless a person is solely concerned with abstract philosophy, which clearly you are not, then they cannot assert the "justice" of any legal proposal without fully evaluating and including the way in which it will work.

Instead, I want to talk factually about what capital punishment is and what it does. To do this in perspective I should dispel the three very wide-spread misconceptions that Michigan is soft on her convicted first-degree murderers, that they are a danger to society either in prison or if released, and that their imprisonment costs large sums of money. The facts which plainly correct these three destructive popular errors are set out in the booklet that we have prepared for you today. It is called "Letters on the Penalty of Death"[2] and includes signed statements by such people as Perry Johnson and others which bring these facts very clearly to your attention.

As to what capital punishment is, I have no desire to be sensational, but I think from my own experience in working with this subject for over a dozen years that many people and perhaps a few of you do not grasp the reality of it. I don't think it would help to show you the picture of Ruth Snyder with the current of the electric chair coursing through her body although I do have that picture here, that clandestine photograph from Sing Sing. I think it might help some, perhaps, to read of the physical torture of the death penalty, which is included as a part of this book entitled *The Case Against Capital Punishment*,[3] which all of you have previously received I am sure. If any of you haven't, we'll make sure that you get one. It's one of the most responsible booklet treatments that I've seen in the 12 years that I've studied the subject. Perhaps the most important to an understanding is to contemplate the prolonged psychological torture and terror which capital punishment inflicts not only on the condemned, but on his or her entirely innocent family.

This barbarity of killing by the State is highlighted by the evidence that is useless in preventing crime, injurious to law enforcement, and harmful to society. It fails to deter murder, it causes the death of innocent persons by occasionally executing the innocent and by inciting additional murders by the mentally disturbed. It is a major obstacle to effective law enforcement, and it is inflicted discriminatorily against blacks, even in the northern states, making the ultimate penalty the ultimate injustice.

DETERRENCE

In talking about the myth of deterrence, what first comes to my mind is Dr. LeMoyne Snyder's statement in his letter for you in this booklet, in which he says, "It seems entirely futile to try to convince some people that capital punishment has no deterrent effect." I think he may be right, based on my experience. There seems to be something about this belief, and I will have to suggest that if any of you feel—intuitively, sort of in your bones—that capital punishment simply *has* to be a deterrent, then I would ask you to carefully consider two vital points before we get into the facts of the matter. The first is that the question is not really whether the death penalty deters. That's not the question. The question is does it deter *better* than life imprisonment? That's the deterrent issue: Does it deter better than life imprisonment? And secondly, if, by chance, your belief is based on how you believe *you* would react, remember that it is very unlikely that you are the sort of person who would plan to commit murder.

As to the facts, I think that briefly stated we need to be quite clear about what we mean by deterrence. From your standpoint, of someone looking for effective law enforcement, deterrence means just one thing—that's fewer murders. Fewer murders, that's what it means. Now if the death penalty deterred murder more than life imprisonment, it would show up in the homicide rate, for with rare exceptions, all homicides in America have been reported since the 1920s. You'll probably be aware there has been a good deal of criticism of criminal statistics; but so far as I know, every one of those studies of criticism has excepted the homicide data from its criticism, very largely. So that data is generally pretty reliable, coming not only from the police but also from the death certificates in the various health departments.

Specifically, if the death penalty deterred, we should expect that there would be a lower homicide rate in the states having the death penalty. More than that, the rate would go up when the penalty is abolished in a state and would go down when the penalty is restored there. In addition to that, in those localities in America where the death penalty is carried out, such as Philadelphia, Chicago and the San Francisco Oakland area, there would be fewer killings near the times of well-publicized executions when any deterrent effect would obviously be greatest. However, 40 years of studies—and I'm talking about simple mathematical, simple arithmetical studies, adding up and taking the average—show that none of these things happen. What the studies show is that there is no correlation between the ups and downs of the homicide rate and the presence or absence of the death penalty. No correlation. It's like an automobile. If your car runs at exactly the same speed regardless of whether the brakes are on or off that's pretty good evidence that the brakes are not working.

The logical implication from this, it seems to me, is clear. If would-be murderers consider the consequences at all, they are either deterred just as much by life imprisonment as they are by the death penalty, or they're planning on not getting caught.

EXECUTING THE INNOCENT

I mentioned that the death penalty not only has not been found to have a deterrent effect, in fact the evidence which exists very clearly points to the fact that it does not; but that it also causes the loss of innocent lives and, notwithstanding great respect for our law enforcement agencies in this state in general, I have to say that conviction of the innocent does occur and that execution makes these ghastly mistakes irrevocable. Professor Hugo Bedau in his well-known book *The Death Penalty in America*[4] pointed out, and documented individually, 74 cases since 1893 in which it's responsibly charged and in most of them proved beyond doubt that persons were wrongfully convicted of criminal homicide in America. Eight of those 74 had been executed. Edward Radin in his book *The Innocents*,[5] and others, specifically identify many additional cases, in addition to the 74 that Bedau found. Both of those books document how difficult it is to uncover the facts when the authorities do not cooperate.

Now, in the booklet which we have prepared for you is given the names of nine persons who since 1910 have been wrongfully convicted of murder in Michigan. Later, for most of them years later, they were all proved innocent and freed. Some of you may remember that one of them, Charles Clark, was compensated three years ago by the legislature for the time he spent in prison for the first-degree murder he did not commit.[6] How many of these men—and the others—would have been executed if we'd had capital punishment? Very probably all of them or most of them if you read the types of cases that they were involved with. And how many other innocent men and women have been convicted "beyond a reasonable doubt" of murder? And how many executed? How often have perjured testimony, mistaken eye-witness identification, and even as evidence was produced to show in the case of Louis Gross, one of those nine Michigan innocents, has a "frame-up" passed for truth? Considering how hard it is to uncover the facts after conviction, let alone after execution, it's obvious that there are many more of these miscarriages of justice than we know about.

I read in your last minutes, your Task Force Minutes of January 27th,[7] the suggestion that these days "safeguards in the judicial system" would prevent such mistakes. It would be hard to explain this to Lindberg Hall, Ephriam Clark and Sceola Kuykendall who in 1961 were convicted of first-degree murder in Detroit and sentenced to prison for life, only to be cleared when the police happened to discover the real murderers about a year later on. The Recorders Court file, a copy of which we received a little while ago,[8] clearly shows that those three were convicted of that capital crime, first-degree murder, based on a combination of perjured testimony and mistaken eye-witness identification. These three, by the way, are in addition to the 9 I mentioned earlier. For an even more recent example, you need look no further than the story in last month's *Detroit News*, the January 22nd feature story beginning, "The so-called eyewitness almost solely responsible for the death sentences given four men for a brutal Albuquerque, New Mexico, murder said today her entire story of the killing was a fabrication."[9] And in this case, as so often happens the perjury was brought to light by the press, not by a law enforcement agency. The fact is that there are no possible, no conceivable, safeguards in the judicial system or safeguards for the judicial system, which could prevent most of these cases from happening. You read them and you find that they are caused almost invariably in one of four ways: 1. Mistaken eye-witness identification, known to all students of the subject as one of the great dangers of our or any judicial system, which it is impossible to have any "rules" to prevent. 2. Perjured testimony, which falls into the same category with a clever and believable perjurer. 3. An occasional frame-up, sometimes by people who are involved in some respects with law enforcement themselves. And finally, and I hope more rarely today, the failure by an over-zealous prosecutor to bring forward evidence of innocence, which it is his sworn duty to do; such as happened in this county some years ago and resulted in the murder conviction of Walter Pecho, who was later pardoned by the governor and declared innocent by the governor, when those very unhappy facts were brought to light.

Now I suppose that we'd say this pretty well tells the story, and pretty well caps it off on the issue of convicting the innocent. But although I'd like to say, Yes, that's the end of it in the interest of time this afternoon, I'll have to say No it doesn't. Because you see, all of these people were proved to have been wrongfully convicted on the objective basis that they didn't do the actual killing. Now you ought to know that first-degree murder involves a lot more than just someone doing the killing, and that these additional areas are areas where the jury in almost every case has the final say-so, which cannot be caught on appeal except very, very rarely. That is on the issue of premeditation, which under the law need only be for the very, very briefest period of time. On the issue of sanity, again a jury question in these cases; and on the issue of self-defense, whether or not the killing was done out of self-defense. Rarely if ever are reversals based on mistakes which are made by the jury in these three areas—and we have no way of knowing how many people were convicted and how many sent to their death on the basis of mistakes in those areas. It may not show up to plague anyone's conscience later because it's pretty hard to discover, but they were none the less innocent of the crime for which they were executed.

ADDITIONAL HOMICIDES

I mentioned also additional homicides and I want to emphasize to you very seriously that capital punishment is known to cause additional murders. These include the so-called "suicide-murder" cases, many of them clinically documented of persons who wanted but feared to take their own lives and so committed murder in order that the state would execute them. This is not at all fanciful. These are cases which have occurred.

The death penalty also causes imitative killings, by the weak-minded who are incited by inevitable sensational publicity of capital trials. One of the most famous examples of this occurred right here in Michigan in the 1920s when Alfred Hotelling brutally murdered a young girl, I believe it was in the eastern part of the state, middle-eastern part of the state, and later testified, which of course is how we know that he was incited to do this by the wake of the publicity of the famous California Hickman trial.

No one knows how many murders are indirectly caused by capital punishment, by the moral lesson it teaches to many persons, which is that killing is a legitimate, even desirable way to solve human problems. As Professors Morris and Hawkins said in their book, published about four years ago in Chicago, called *The Honest Politician's Guide to Crime Control*, "If we are to be sincere in our efforts to reduce violence, there's one type of violence that we can with complete certainty eliminate and that is the killing of criminals by the state. The question is," and I think this is very interesting, "The question is, Will people learn to respect life better by threat or by example? And the uniform answer of history, comparative studies and experience is that man is an emulative animal."

This is all confirmed additionally by a letter in this booklet for you from Dr. Albert Silverman, who is the Chairman of the Department of Psychiatry at the University of Michigan Medical School: Among a number of important points, he says, "What bothers me as a psychiatrist . . . is the fact that there seems to be no recognition of the fact that the only thing capital punishment accomplishes is to *increase* the propensity for murder. As you know, we carry in our society a number of borderline personalities, who depending upon social sanctions will tend to act in one way or other. Since capital punishment legitimizes killing as a solution to problems some of these individuals are actually incited to violence." And he goes on, not to quote him entirely, you can read it, but he says, "Others murder as a wish for suicide. Some murderers have scolded those in authority for denying them the death penalty. Patients have stated explicitly that they are too chicken to kill themselves. They kill in order to be killed by the state. These are sick people. The death penalty is an invitation, not a deterrent to them."

I think it can be capped off pretty well with the famous statement Bernard Shaw made, a number of years ago. He said, "Murder and capital punishment are not opposites that cancel one another, but similars that breed their kind."

IMPAIRING LAW ENFORCEMENT

I'm sure that many of you, perhaps most of you, are very concerned about the effect which capital punishment may have upon law enforcement and are dedicated to doing whatever you can to improve the effectiveness of law enforcement, or at least, at the very least, to prevent placing any impediment in its way. And so I want to emphasize how severe a barrier the death penalty is to law enforcement: particularly by obstructing that certainty and swiftness of conviction and punishment that is society's best deterrent to crime.

Experience shows that juries often refuse to convict when the defendant's life may be at stake, and that where penalty is life imprisonment, more convictions are possible with less delays. Now this concept of juries refusing to convict when the penalty is or may be death has been long known to students of criminology and it's called "jury nullification." That is the term that is universally applied to this phenomenon. It's been known to exist, it's been combatted for years, in fact, the practice grew up early in our history, after they divided murder into first and second degrees to try to get away from the problem, they had to start excluding people from the juries who had any kind of objection to capital punishment. If you sit under the jury selection process and you don't think capital punishment is really a very good idea, you're off the jury automatically as they say "for cause." Well, the Supreme Court struck that down a few years ago in the *Witherspoon* case,[10] and so today it's no longer possible to do that. You can't exclude someone from the jury because they have some possible objections or doubts about the propriety of the death penalty. That means that those people will be on the juries. Now, there have been some polls taken about whether people are in favor or not of the death penalty and they received some publicity. Some of them are not too scientific, but they still get the publicity. But one poll that has received very little publicity is the Louis Harris Poll. I have a copy of the poll results right here from Lou Harris and they point out—and this is, by the way, just a 1973 poll, the poll of June 14, 1973—which shows that even if guilt were proven, almost one-third of the American people are not sure that they could vote to convict if the defendant would be executed. Now, you think we had trouble with jury nullification *before*, what do you think is going to happen to law enforcement if you have capital punishment now? Certainly it's much better that two murderers go to prison for life than that one be executed and that the other go free. But that's what you're faced with.

Secondly, I have to say, and as a lawyer perhaps I'm not as cautious as I ought to be but I feel compelled to say anyway, that the evidence we have strongly indicates that similar considerations apply at the appellate level to appellate judges: That judges sometimes distort the course of the law itself, in their sincere efforts to apply it justly to an appellant whose life is at stake. As Mr. Justice Robert Jackson of the U.S. Supreme Court, as some of you may remember, the prosecutor for America at the Nuremburg Trials, candidly admitted, "When the penalty is death, we, like state court judges, are tempted to strain the evidence and even in close cases the law, in order to give doubtfully condemned men another chance." James Bennett, lawyer and former director of the Federal Bureau of Prisons, testified before Congress very bluntly in 1968 on this point as follows—I'm quoting him—"At bottom the retention of the death penalty has led to all sorts of controversial, not to say inconsistent and erratic decisions of our courts on such things as mental responsibility for crime, use of confessions, admissibility of evidence, arrest and arraignment procedures, and so on." Such results, I submit, are in the very nature of things when judges who deeply value human life are immersed in an atmosphere so incompatible with the cool, rational processes of thought that are necessary, absolutely necessary, for the best application and development of the law.

In addition, because you're dealing with a subject that costs a lot of money, and not in any sense to equate money with human life, I want to tell you that, as is partly pointed out in this booklet for you by the data we have and the statements which we have collected, that frankly life imprisonment is financially much cheaper than the death penalty, thus saving a good deal of money, which, as I'm sure you know is desperately needed to effectively fight crime. Perry Johnson pointed out last March that the prisoners serving time in Michigan at that time for first-degree murder, when you average them out, were financially carrying their own weight. This should not be surprising for as the internationally known criminologist Thorsten Sellin pointed out in his famous book on *The Death Penalty*, "In a well-organized penal system murderers as a group can undoubtedly earn their keep." That's pretty much the status quo, and it's also confirmed, again by letter, from Perry Johnson, in this booklet for you.

On the other hand, both the litigation costs and the prison costs increase greatly where you have capital punishment. When the defendant's life is at stake the trial takes a lot longer, is more fully fought out at every conceivable level and point, from the jury selection to the last desperate appeal. I can tell you that the appellate courts give especially careful consideration to appeals by condemned persons, thus involving substantial expensive judicial time and court staff time. The cost of all this, including judge, lawyer time, courtroom space, security arrangements, stenographers' costs, and printing briefs and records can run tremendously high. Of course, usually the government must pay the cost of the defense as well as the cost of prosecution because the defendant is indigent. The Sirhan and Manson murder trials alone are said to have cost the people of the state of California a million dollars. Now that's the litigation costs.

If you look at the prison costs, I'd like to emphasize how expensive they are; and without going into some letters and materials on cost accounting, let me just repeat what Richard McGee, administrator of the California correctional system, stated about ten years ago in a paper published in *Federal*

Probation. He said, "The actual costs of execution, the cost of operating the super-maximum security condemned unit, the years spent by some inmates in condemned status and a pro-rata share of top-level prison officials' time spent in administering the unit, add up to a cost substantially greater than the cost to retain them in prison for the rest of their lives."

RACIAL DISCRIMINATION

Now the subject of racial discrimination has been mentioned by Kirby Holmes, with the appeal or suggestion that we have come a long way in the last 20 years in our search for racial justice. However, I'll have to say that I don't see, myself, where the problem of racial justice has been solved. Revival of the death penalty, in practice, I'm very much afraid would severely aggravate racial tension, because, and this is very important, the rate of execution of blacks in this country far exceeds the proportion of capital crimes committed by black defendants. By way of background you should know that of all persons executed in America since 1930, over 53 percent have been black, although blacks have made up only about ten percent of the population. Leaving aside the experience of the southern states, which I can assure you in some cases is staggering, let's look at a few states in the north where, as was pointed out in the Washington Research Project booklet here, the pattern of discrimination shows up dramatically even after sentencing. "A study of commutations in Pennsylvania between 1914 and 1948 revealed that whites were nearly twice as likely as blacks to have their sentences commuted. A similar study in New Jersey found almost precisely the same pattern. Whites were twice as likely as blacks to have death sentences commuted. In Ohio, over a ten year period, 78% of blacks sentenced to death were actually executed while only 51% of the whites were." If you want to look at the data of death rows today in a number of states, I believe that in North or South Carolina, and in some of the others, you find a majority of those on death row are black. Of course it's being appealed to the U.S. Supreme Court as most of you I think realize, but they have been convicted under new death penalty provisions of doubtful constitutionality. All I can say is that despite recent progress toward racial justice in America, and thank God for it, it still is wishful thinking to assert that it can't possibly happen now.

PROTECTING SOCIETY

Well, finally, and again as it has been pointed out in this booklet in more detail than I am going to give you, society, particularly Michigan society, is amply protected by life imprisonment for first-degree murder. The data clearly shows this, and I am sure Mr. McConnell could explain this to you and tell you the facts even better than I could. In any event that is spelled out in detail in the booklet there.

COMMENT ON ARGUMENTS

Now before entertaining any questions which you have, I want to comment upon the arguments which your minutes of January 27th show were advanced in favor of "limited use of capital punishment." I think that would be fair, and it might answer some questions that some of you might have. First of all there is no such a thing as "limited" use of capital punishment. A person is either killed or they're not.

The first point that was made, and I am quoting here, "1. Criminals are now informally practicing capital punishment when they murder; the law should have equal tools in the fight against criminals." The answer, as I have shown, is that capital punishment weakens the tools of law enforcement.

"2. Whether or not capital punishment is a deterrent to crime, it is fitting punishment for certain criminal acts." In other words, even if it doesn't deter it is still fitting. Well, of course you get into the area of moral judgement or justice I know, but I want to ask this: Fitting for whom? Is it fitting for the innocent family of the condemned? His family who go through the torture and the suffering of it, the psychological torture of it? Is it fitting for the family of the victim? Of course it won't restore the victim's life, won't bring them back. And the family may not even want it. In fact the mayor, former mayor, of the city of Lansing's daughter was brutally murdered in a rather sensational case locally; and a lot of publicity was connected with it. A tragic, tragic thing. The culprit was never found. A couple of years later the newspaper, as it did occasionally, had some interviews on the subject, and, in a feature story about this tragedy, it quoted them as saying that now after having gone through this they really preferred that the murderer was not found, because they had just been through too much already, and this would just revive it all. Well, is it fitting for those victims of the murderers which capital punishment incites? Obviously that doesn't seem to be very fitting for them, because without capital punishment they would still be alive. Is it fitting for those executed by mistake? Is it fitting even for the executioner? The most experienced, I might say the "greatest" executioner in modern American-English history just published his memoirs in England last year. As published in his memoirs, he very clearly stated that he did not believe capital punishment was a deterrent. Mr. Pierrepoint's book I think is available in this country now. And finally is it fitting for those people who thirst for vengeance, who as Darrow said "simply love the thought of somebody being killed?" I don't think that that emotion, which perhaps exists to some extent in most of us, should be encouraged or pandered to. In other words, in order to determine whether or not something is fitting you can't take it abstractly. You have to say, Is it fitting in the way that it is actually going to work and that history shows that it works?

Well, more quickly, "3. The increasing trend toward calculated murder (to eliminate witnesses and criminal competitors or to pursue political goals) requires stronger sanctions than were previously needed." First of all I question based on this, if such a trend, any greater trend, toward calculated murder exists. Except possibly in the political area: but the political area is exactly that area where capital punishment is most likely to be an incitement to murder, because those politically motivated are often seeking the sensation of publicity and even martyrdom.

"4. Public frustration with failure to stop serious crimes demands a strong response." Strong is the wrong word. Effective, "demands an effective response." And certainly that should include informing the public; and clearly from what I said you know, or I am sure more of you are sure now, that capital punishment is not an effective way.

"5." and this is very distressing to me, "Certain hardened criminals are immune to either deterrence or rehabilitation and should receive the ultimate sanction." Even if abstractly this were so, and I am not going to argue about that, Who is going to pick them? Who is going to decide on those people who are beyond rehabilitation? The so-called mafia type hardly ever is caught, hardly ever prosecuted. So we are not talking much about that sort of murderer. Going back into history, how about Moses? He murdered the Egyptian before he led the Jews into the promised land. What about Paul? If he was not a murderer he was very definitely a murderer's helper before God made him an Apostle. To become more modern, what about Robert Stroud: a double murderer: two brutal murders: the "birdman of Alcatraz," who later made outstanding contributions to ornithology? How about Nathan Leopold? No one ever thought he could possibly be rehabilitated or reformed and yet he was, and made significant contributions to sociology. Paul Crump, down in Chicago, who was described first as a beast in human form and yet by some process, no one is entirely sure how, with the help of an outstanding warden at the Cook County Jail, he did become reformed. And what about the lesser known people who are described so well in Don Thurston's letter to you in this booklet? He is a member and former lifer examiner on our own Michigan Parole Board. Well, I think it's implicit in Christianity and other religions that no human being is totally beyond all hope of reformation; and I think that is my answer to the fifth argument.

"6. There are enough safeguards in the judicial system so that only those few most deserving of capital punishment would actually receive that sanction." I think I've covered that.

And finally "7. If procedures can be devised to prevent discrimination in the application of capital punishment (against minorities or the poor), then the sanction might be more generally acceptable." I say, When that day comes! When you can show, when society can show that it has accomplished those procedures to prevent discrimination and that they work. That's the time to bring that argument up, not before.

Well, finally, I'm sorry Kirby had to leave, but I cannot help but respond to the assertion he made that we are really talking about two different things.

That I am talking about apples and oranges. This data about the way human beings act is not ancient, but you know it comes right up to recent years. Sure some of it goes back 20, 30, 40 years. But it is pure speculation and certainly contrary to known experience to say people react differently today, basically, than they did 10, 20, 30 or 40 years ago. Human nature is not something which in most of our experience changes that fast. His idea that it is significant that we have had a marked increase in our homicide rate and that no one has been executed since 1967, it seems to me has no significance to the deterrent argument at all. I am sure most of you realize that just because you prove the existence of a correlation does not in any way imply the existence of cause and effect. Not in any way. Like they used to say in college: Railroad trains *must* cause babies because the people who live down by the railroad tracks have larger families! Of course there is no causal relationship. Or the idea that watching scantily clad beautiful women causes the hair to fall out because you observe that everybody in the first 12 rows of the burlesque theatre is bald. You know that that is a correlation, but obviously there is no causal relationship. That is the same thing here.

On the other hand the data which I've been showing is the reverse of that, which is different. It may be a paradox, but it is true: If you show the absence of a correlation that usually or frequently also tends to prove the absence of causation. For example, if those people down by the railroad tracks didn't have larger families, but in fact all had smaller families than average, that would pretty clearly tend to prove that railroad trains *did not cause* larger families. See what I mean? That kind of argument doesn't have any validity at all. It's not logical and it doesn't apply to the situation today.

That pretty well concludes the presentation that I wanted to make to you today, but I want to say if you have any factual questions, if I cannot answer them to your satisfaction I will try to get the information, because I think we are in touch with most of the people in the United states who are the leaders in bringing together this data, and fighting it out in other places in the country, and in Washington. I want to thank you for your very excellent attention.

QUESTIONS

MR. GEERLINGS: I just have a question.

MR. WANGER: Sure.

MR. GEERLINGS: Do you personally feel that a man has a right to take a life to protect not only his life but his property?

MR. WANGER: I'm not sure about the property. I suspect . . . Well, legally no. The legal answer is no. You're talking about a moral question: Suppose you try to take my pipe. That's my property. "Bang!" (pointing at Mr. Geerlings).

MR. GEERLINGS: O.K.

MR. WANGER: Suppose I've saved all my life and . . .

MR. GEERLINGS: Take it the other way. Suppose you came into my house, and pulled a gun on me, and took something, stole something, and you were on your way out and I picked up a shotgun and I shot you as you were going out the door. Now do I have justification there? Having been assaulted?

MR. WANGER: Well . . .

MR. GEERLINGS: Or if I have a shotgun and a guy comes in and hits me over the head with a gun or stabs me with a knife and takes the goods out of the cash register and he's on his way out and I blast him in the back, shooting him going out of the door. Do you feel as strongly there in these acts about the preservation of life as you do about capital punishment?

MR. WANGER: First of all, you're asking for moral judgments on these things, and I will tell you my own individual view as long as you will understand that I in no way necessarily speak for all of the members of the Michigan

Committee Against Capital Punishment. I'd say frankly, I don't see any connection between those sorts of activities and whether or not we should have the death penalty. It seems to me quite a difference, it would make quite a difference, as to what your intent was. Did you intend to kill that person when you pulled a shotgun and pulled the trigger, or were you merely trying to stop them? Were you aiming high, in other words, or were you aiming down at their legs? Did you shoot to kill, or were you aiming down at their legs to stop them? Intent plays a very large part here. And I would think you could make a very strong case that you have the right to use whatever force is reasonably necessary to stop someone; but, no, you don't have the right to kill them, unless you have to preserve yourself, ordinarily.

MR. GEERLINGS: O.K., I guess I'm trying to draw a correlation between those who oppose—are adamant to any change—against any form of capital punishment, and their attitude toward the preservation of life in other life situations. And I guess there are some of those people who firmly believe that regardless of the situation—somebody comes in and physically assaults you, sexually assaults you, no matter how hideously it may be, you know. Now, I understand something like that.

MR. WANGER: Well, I guess all I can say is that our group includes all sorts of people, and you've heard some of their names, and these people would have all sorts of answers to the questions you've just put. I would have to say that as a practical matter I think most people who have joined our Committee, on the executive committee or have helped us, have done it on the basis of these facts that I've been talking about. And they don't know the facts about how many people break in, and how many of them are killed and all that. But they do know the facts about what happens when you have the death penalty. Yes, Senator?

MR. RICHARDSON: We've got some figures here showing that, well not a majority, I guess, but more people do than don't want to have some form of capital punishment. Kirby Holmes' initial argument was if I recall that although he's in favor of capital punishment, all he's been trying to do is to give the people a chance to vote on this—because that's all we can do. How do you answer this? Do people or do they not have the right to say whether they want capital punishment?

MR. WANGER: Well, very clearly. First of all, there isn't any question about the legal right, if they get enough signatures, to put it on the ballot, if they follow the law. No question about that. But I'll say two things: Number one, uninformed public opinion has no moral value at all.

A VOICE: Right!

MR. WANGER: And secondly, the public is appallingly misinformed and uninformed. I've had a clipping service for two years for our Committee. Every story in every Michigan newspaper that mentions the death penalty one way or the other, I get. Ninety percent is for Kirby Holmes and others stirring things up for the death penalty; maybe ten percent, although maybe it's getting a little bit better, but about ten percent even mentioning that there are facts on the other side . . .

MR. RICHARDSON: But couldn't you say that about any question that's presented to the people.

MR. WANGER: Well of course that's immaterial. But maybe yes; but so far as I know, though, this has always been the case with the death penalty. And I'm not . . . maybe years ago I would have attacked the papers and the press for this . . . but I understand a lot more about their problems of deadlines, that their boss can't pay them to go study up on things, maybe, I understand. Maybe this is true in other areas, but of course it's no justification. It's just an explanation. That may explain it, but it doesn't justify it.

MR. GEERLINGS: "State Government," I've just received this over the week-end, says "Death penalty laws were enacted in 8 more states in 1974 for a total of 29 which have restored capital punishment since the U.S. Supreme Court ruled on the matter in 1972." If the preponderance of evidence, as you seem to believe, is so overwhelmingly in favor of abolition of the death penalty, because there are no benefits at all to be derived, by the public, by reinstating the death penalty, how do you account for this overwhelming reaction on the part of states in enacting death penalty laws?

MR. WANGER: Well, there's two sides to this coin. By the way, it's 30 states now. The thing is this. There are two sides to the coin. First of all, all the states which have restored the death penalty have restored it in a much narrower form than they had it before. Every one of them. There may be one exception, I forget which one it is. Secondly, all the original abolition states, including Michigan which was historically the first, have held the line. Third, even though it's been two and a half years since *Furman* there's an additional dozen states—subtract thirty from fifty states—there's an additional ten, or dozen, states in there which have, even though they've had two and a half years, said, No, we're still not going to restore it. I look at that side of the coin and I say, considering the politically sensational nature of it—it's so easy to ride this horse, it's just so easy to ride it politically—considering that, considering that the Supreme Court struck down *their* statute, you know, which of course we didn't have in Michigan, so it didn't change our operation but it did change theirs, I can see how that would have happened. So I look at the other side of the coin and I think that there's clear evidence that people in some cases, and particularly some of the leaders such as yourselves, are beginning to realize the very questionable value of the death penalty.

MR. MCCONNELL: Are there any more questions? It's been a pretty full day, Gene. I want to say thank you for your time. And I know . . . I can imagine that you'll have opportunity to speak further as will Mr. Holmes at some of our future public meetings. And you can be sure we'll welcome that.

MR. WANGER: Thank you.

NOTES

1. State Representative Kirby Holmes, the previous speaker favoring capital punishment.

2. *Letters on the Penalty of Death,* compiled by Michigan Committee Against Capital Punishment, 1202 Michigan National Tower, Lansing, Michigan, 48933, 1975.

3. *The Case Against Capital Punishment,* by The Washington Research Project, Washington, D.C., 1971, 68 pp.

4. Hugo A. Bedau, ed., *The Death Penalty in America,* rev. ed. New York: Anchor Books, 1967, 584 pp.

5. Edward D. Radin, *The Innocents,* New York: Wm. Morrow & Co., 1964.

6. By Michigan Public Act No. 1 of 1972; see also vol. 389, page 200 of the Michigan Supreme Court Reports, for an account.

7. Minutes, Capital Punishment Task Force, January 27, 1975, p. 2.

8. Detroit, Michigan, Recorder's Court File No. A-104699.

9. *The Detroit News,* January 22, 1975, p. 1, col. 1, paragraph 1.

10. *Witherspoon v. Illinois,* 391 U.S. 510 (1968).

8. Death Ban Defended

For Release Monday, April 7, 1975.

The Michigan Committee Against Capital Punishment today urged the state's Criminal Justice Commission to oppose restoring the death penalty. Speaking to Commission members in Detroit, committee co-chairman Eugene G. Wanger said, "The evidence clearly shows that capital punishment is useless in fighting crime, is harmful to society and damages effective law enforcement. If our historic abolition state adopts it now, it could have international consequences."

Michigan in 1846 was the first English-speaking government to abolish capital punishment for murder and lesser crimes, and has never restored it. Later other countries, including Canada and England, followed Michigan's lead.

"It fails to deter murder," Wanger stated. "Whether you are a policeman, prison guard or plain citizen, the facts show you are no safer from being a victim of homicide where they have the death penalty."

Further, the innocent are sometimes convicted and execution makes such mistakes irrevocable. Wanger named 13 innocent persons convicted of murder in Michigan since 1910, who years later were proved innocent and freed. Most had been convicted by perjured testimony or mistaken identification. Very likely there are more, he pointed out, because it is hard to uncover the facts, especially when authorities do not cooperate.

"Capital punishment severely impairs that certainty and swiftness of conviction and punishment which is society's best deterrent to crime," Wanger added. "Experience shows that juries often refuse to convict when the penalty is death, and that where you have life imprisonment more convictions are possible with less delays."

9. Testimony of Eugene G. Wanger, Co-Chairman of the Michigan Committee Against Capital Punishment Before the Michigan Advisory Commission on Criminal Justice April 7, 1975

Mr. Chairman, Ladies and Gentlemen:

My name is Eugene G. Wanger and I am co-chairman, with Tom Downs, of the Michigan Committee Against Capital Punishment. We are a volunteer citizens' group which organized over two years ago to oppose the restoration of the death penalty in our historic abolition state.

Our executive committee includes Arthur Brandstatter, head of the School of Criminal Justice at Michigan State University, D. Hale Brake, former prosecutor and distinguished Michigan public servant, William Cahalan, Wayne County prosecutor, Bishop Dwight Loder, Methodist Bishop of Michigan, Perry Johnson, director of the Michigan Department of Corrections, John A. Hannah and others equally dedicated to the good of our state and country.

We ask you to strongly recommend against restoring the death penalty for any crime. We urge you to help inform an appallingly uninformed public of the compelling reasons why. We submit that you not only have a unique opportunity, but a signal responsibility, to help lay this issue to rest.

Putting this useless, dangerous and sensational issue on the ballot would consume an immense amount of time, attention, effort and money which could otherwise be used to effectively fight and prevent crime. It would successfully divert public and official attention away from effective ways of strengthening Michigan's criminal law and law enforcement system. Considering the seriousness of the crime problem, this would be a tragedy.

The barbarity of killing by the state is highlighted by the evidence that it is useless in fighting crime, is harmful to society, and damages effective law enforcement:

1. It fails to deter murder better than life imprisonment. Whether you are a policeman, prison guard or plain citizen, the evidence clearly shows that you are not safer where they have the death penalty.
2. It causes the deaths of innocent persons, by occasionally executing the innocent and by inciting additional killings by the mentally disturbed.
3. It is a major barrier to effective law enforcement, by severely impairing that *certainty* and *swiftness* of conviction and punishment which is society's best deterrent to crime.
4. It is inflicted discriminatorily against blacks—even in Northern states— severely aggravating racial tensions and making the ultimate penalty the ultimate injustice.

Let us consider these reasons one at a time.

DETERRENCE

In talking about the myth of deterrence, what first comes to mind is a statement of Dr. LeMoyne Snyder, former Medicolegal Director of the Michigan State Police and internationally known expert on homicide, that "It seems entirely futile to try to convince some people that capital punishment has no deterrent effect." If any of you feel that capital punishment simply *has* to be a deterrent, then I ask you to carefully consider two vital points before we get into the facts: First, the question is not really whether the death penalty deters, but whether it deters *better* than life imprisonment. Second, if your belief is based on how you believe *you* would react, remember that it is very unlikely that you are the sort of person we are talking about deterring.

As to the facts, we need to be quite clear about what we mean by deterrence. From the standpoint of effective law enforcement, deterrence means just one thing—fewer murders. If the death penalty deterred murder more than life imprisonment, it would show up in the homicide rate, for with rare exceptions all homicides in America have been reported since the 1920s. Specifically, if the death penalty deterred, there should be a lower homicide rate in the states having the death penalty; the rate would go up when the penalty is abolished in a state and go down when it is restored there; and in those localities in America where the death penalty is carried out—such as Philadelphia, Chicago and the San Francisco area—there would be fewer killings near the times of well-publicized executions when any deterrent effect would be greatest.

However, 40 years of studies—and perhaps no subject in criminology has been studied more—show that none of these things happen. What they show is that there is no correlation between the ups and downs of homicide and the presence or absence of the death penalty. It's like an automobile. If your car runs at exactly the same speed regardless of whether its brakes are on or off that's pretty good evidence that the brakes are not working.

Similar studies of police and prison guard safety reach the same conclusion. As Perry Johnson said,

> One argument I have heard for capital punishment is that it is needed to protect the officers in the prison, since the man who has murdered and is serving first-degree life has nothing to fear from murdering again. I can only say that our experience seems to refute this very clearly. We have had but one corrections officer murdered in the history of the Michigan prison system, to my knowledge, as compared with some other states which have capital punishment but which have had many officers murdered by inmates. The one murder of the officer, which occurred last November, was not committed by a man serving first-degree life.

The logical implication from all this is clear: If would-be murderers consider the consequences at all, they are either deterred just as much by life imprisonment as they are by the death penalty, or they are planning on not getting caught.

EXECUTING THE INNOCENT

There is probably nothing in the universe of moral possibilities more horrible than the execution of the wrong man or woman. Yet conviction of the innocent does occur and execution makes these ghastly mistakes irrevocable. Professor Hugo Bedau in his well-known book *The Death Penalty in America* individually documents 74 cases since 1893 in which it's responsibly charged and in most of them proved beyond doubt that persons were wrongfully convicted of criminal homicide in America. Eight of the 74 had been executed. Edward Radin in his book *The Innocents*, and others, specifically identify many additional cases. Both of those books document how difficult it is to uncover the facts when the authorities do not cooperate.

In Michigan since 1910 at least 13 persons have been wrongfully convicted of murder. Later, for most of them years later, they were all proved innocent and freed. They are Robert MacGregor, Alexander Ripan, Lloyd Prevost, Vance Hardy, Gerald Crowden, Louis Gross, "Paget," Willie Calloway, Walter Pecho, Ephriam Clark, Lindberg Hall, Sceola Kuykendall and Charles Clark. Some of you may remember that one of them, Charles Clark, was compensated three years ago by the legislature for the time he spent in prison for the first-degree murder he did not commit. How many of these men would have been executed if Michigan had had the death penalty? How many other innocent men and women have been convicted "beyond a reasonable doubt" of murder? And how many executed? How often have perjured testimony, mistaken eye-witness identification, and even as evidence was produced to show in the case of Louis Gross, has a "frame-up" passed for truth? Considering how hard it is to uncover the facts after conviction, let alone after execution, it is obvious that there are many more of these miscarriages of justice than we know.

I read in your Commission Task Force Minutes of January 27th, the suggestion that these days "safeguards in the judicial system" would prevent such mistakes. It would be hard to explain this to Lindberg Hall, Ephriam Clark and Sceola Kuykendall who in 1961 were convicted of first-degree murder in Detroit and sentenced to prison for life, only to be cleared when the police happened to discover the real murderers about a year later on. For an even more recent example, you need look no further than the Detroit News' January 22nd feature story beginning,

> The so-called eyewitness almost solely responsible for the death sentences given four men for a brutal Albuquerque, New Mexico, murder said today her entire story of the killing was a fabrication.

And in this case, as so often happens the perjury was brought to light by the press, not by a law enforcement agency.

The fact is that there are no possible or conceivable safeguards in or for the judicial system which could prevent most of these cases from happening. They are caused almost invariably in one of four ways: Mistaken eye-witness identification, known to all students of the subject as one of the great dangers of our or any judicial system, which it is impossible to have any "rules" to prevent. Or perjured testimony, which falls into the same category with a clever and believable perjurer. Then there is an occasional frame-up, sometimes by people who are involved in law enforcement themselves. Finally, the failure by an over-zealous prosecutor to bring forward evidence of innocence.

And there is more: Because these people were proved to have been wrongfully convicted on the objective basis that they didn't do the actual killing. Now first-degree murder involves more than doing the killing. It always involves premeditation, and often the questions of sanity and self-defense. In these three difficult and usually subjective areas the jury in almost every case has the final say-so, which cannot be caught on appeal except very, very rarely. Seldom if ever are reversals based on mistakes which are made by the jury in these areas—and we have no way of knowing how many people were convicted and how many sent to their deaths on the basis of mistakes in these areas.

ADDITIONAL HOMICIDES

Capital punishment causes additional homicides. These include the so-called "suicide-murder" cases, many of them clinically documented of persons who wanted but feared to take their own lives and so committed murder in order that the state would execute them. They include imitative killings, by the weak-minded who are incited by the inevitable sensational publicity of capital trials. One of the most famous examples occurred right here in Michigan in the 1920s when Alfred Hotelling brutally murdered a young girl, incited to do it by the publicity of the famous California Hickman trial.

No one knows how many murders are indirectly caused by the moral lesson capital punishment teaches to many: That killing is a legitimate, even desirable solution to human problems. As Professors Morris and Hawkins said in their book, *The Honest Politician's Guide to Crime Control,*

> If... we are to be sincere in our efforts to reduce violence, there is one type of violence that we can with complete certainty eliminate. That is the killing of criminals by the state. The question is, Will people learn to respect life better by threat or by example? And the uniform answer of history, comparative studies, and experience is that man is an emulative animal . . .

Dr. Albert Silverman, Chairman of the Department of Psychiatry of the University of Michigan Medical School, put it this way,

> . . . what bothers me as a psychiatrist and educator is the fact that there seems to be no recognition of the fact that the *only* thing capital punishment accomplishes is to *increase* the propensity for murder.
>
> As you know we carry in our society a number of borderline personalities, who, depending on social sanctions will tend to act in one way or other.

Since capital punishment legitimizes killing as a solution to problems some of these individuals are actually incited to violence.

The model of our leaders sanctioning killing can and has led individuals to state—"our leaders do it, why can't I." (Surely you have heard this type of response in another context as a leader is involved in some conflict of interest or other wrong doing. The public response is obvious.)

Others murder as a wish for suicide. Some murderers have scolded those in authority for denying them the death penalty. Patients have stated explicitly that they are "too chicken" to kill themselves. They kill in order to be killed by the state. These are sick people. The death penalty is an invitation, not a deterrent to them.

As Bernard Shaw said, "Murder and capital punishment are not opposites that cancel one another, but similars that breed their kind."

IMPAIRING LAW ENFORCEMENT

I know that you are dedicated to doing whatever you can to improve the effectiveness of proper law enforcement, or at least to prevent placing any impediment in its way. I therefore want to specially emphasize how severe a barrier the death penalty is to law enforcement: particularly by obstructing the certainty and speed of conviction and punishment that is society's best deterrent to crime.

Experience shows that juries often refuse to convict when the defendant's life may be at stake, and that where the penalty is life imprisonment, more convictions are possible with less delays. Now this has been long known to students of criminology and it's called "jury nullification." It's been combatted for years: in fact, the practice grew up early in our history of excluding people from the juries who had any kind of objection to capital punishment. If you didn't think capital punishment was really a very good idea, you were off the jury automatically "for cause." Well, the Supreme Court struck that practice down a few years ago in the *Witherspoon* case, so that today it's no longer possible.

That means that those people will be on the juries. How will they vote today? The Louis Harris Poll, and I have a copy of the poll results right here—his poll of June 14, 1973—shows that even if guilt were proven, almost one-third of the American people are not sure that they could vote to convict if the defendant would be executed. Considering the trouble we had with jury nullification before, what will happen to law enforcement if we have capital punishment now? Surely it is better that two murderers go to prison for life than that one be executed and the other go free.

In addition, capital punishment causes prolonged delays. When the defendant's life is at stake the trial takes much longer, is more fully fought out at every conceivable level and point, from before jury selection to the last desperate appeal. The stakes compel it, and the publicity invites it. The appellate courts give especially careful consideration to appeals by condemned persons, thus involving substantial expensive judicial and court staff time. The cost of all this, including judge and lawyer time, courtroom space, security arrangements, stenographers' costs, and printing briefs and records can run tremendously high. The Sirhan and Manson murder trials alone are said to have cost the taxpayers of California a million dollars. Of course, usually the government must pay the cost of the defense as well as the cost of prosecution because the defendant is indigent. In this connection, Dr. LeMoyne Snyder recently said,

> Within fifty miles of where I live in California Juan Corona was convicted of murdering twenty-five persons and within recent years there have been several other multiple murders—one of which also involved the killing of the trial judge. Incidentally, the cost to the state for the trial of at least three of these murders amounted to over a million dollars each.
>
> Nothing comparable to this ever happened during the years I was Medicolegal Director of the Michigan State Police from 1930 to 1948. Nearly all persons charged with first-degree murder pled guilty and the trial was over in a day. In fact I recall that the Michigan Supreme Court granted habeas corpus in more than twenty cases where the murder, the apprehension of the killer, the arraignment, the guilty plea and incarceration for life in the state

prison all occurred on the same day. While we don't approve of "quick justice" carried out in this fashion it does illustrate the contrast to what happens in capital punishment states where virtually no-one ever pleads guilty to first degree murder.

Further, appellate judges sometimes distort the course of the law itself, in their sincere efforts to apply it justly to an appellant whose life is at stake. As Mr. Justice Robert Jackson of the U. S. Supreme Court candidly admitted, "When the penalty is death, we, like state court judges, are tempted to strain the evidence and even in close cases the law, in order to give doubtfully condemned men another chance." And James Bennett, lawyer and former director of the Federal Bureau of Prisons, bluntly testified before Congress in 1968 that,

> At bottom the retention of the death penalty has led to all sorts of contro-
> versial, not to say inconsistent and erratic decisions of our courts on such
> things as mental responsibility for crime, use of confessions, admissibility of
> evidence, arrest and arraignment procedures, and so on.

He believes that we might not have a number of those decisions were it not for the fact that the death penalty was involved. Yet such results are in the very nature of things when judges who deeply value human life are immersed in an atmosphere so incompatible with the cool, rational processes of thought that are necessary for the best application and development of the law.

One final point on capital punishment and law enforcement: its cost. Surprising as it is to the advocates of execution, life imprisonment is financially much cheaper than the death penalty, thus saving money which is desperately needed to effectively fight crime.

Perry Johnson pointed out last March (1974) that the prisoners then serving time in Michigan for first-degree murder, when you average them out, were financially carrying their own weight. This should not be surprising for as the internationally known criminologist Thorsten Sellin pointed out in his famous book on *The Death Penalty*, "In a well-organized penal system murderers as a group can undoubtedly earn their keep."

On the other hand, both the litigation costs and the prison costs greatly increase where you have capital punishment. I've already discussed the litigation costs. As to just the prison costs, here is what Richard McGee, administrator of the California correctional system, stated about ten years ago in a paper published in Federal Probation:

> The actual costs of execution, the cost of operating the super-maximum security condemned unit, the years spent by some inmates in condemned status and a pro-rata share of top-level prison officials' time spent in administering the unit, add up to a cost substantially greater than the cost to retain them in prison for the rest of their lives.

RACIAL DISCRIMINATION

Revival of the death penalty, in practice, would severely aggravate racial tension, because the rate of execution of blacks in this country far exceeds the proportion of capital crimes committed by black defendants. Of all persons executed in America since 1930, over 53% have been black, although blacks have made up only about ten percent of the population. Leaving aside evidence from the Southern states, let's look at three states in the North where, as was pointed out by the Washington Research Project, the pattern of discrimination shows up dramatically even after sentencing:

> A study of commutations in Pennsylvania between 1914 and 1948 revealed that whites were nearly twice as likely as blacks to have their sentences commuted. A similar study in New Jersey found almost precisely the same pattern. Whites were twice as likely as blacks to have death sentences commuted. In Ohio, over a ten year period, 78% of blacks sentenced to death were actually executed while only 51% of the whites were.

Despite recent progress toward racial justice, it is wishful thinking to assert that it can't possibly happen again.

COMMENT ON ARGUMENTS

Now before entertaining your questions, I want to comment upon two arguments which your Minutes of January 27th show were advanced in favor of capital punishment. The first is,

> Whether or not capital punishment is a deterrent to crime, it is fitting punishment for certain criminal acts.

I want to ask, Fitting for whom? Is it fitting for the innocent family of the condemned? His or her family who go through the terrible psychological torture and suffering of it? Is it fitting for the family of the victim? Of course it won't restore the victim's life. And the family may not even want it. In fact, I know a recent Michigan case where a family's daughter was brutally murdered; and a lot of publicity was connected with it. A tragic, tragic thing. The killer was never found. A couple of years later the newspaper, as it occasionally did, had some interviews on the subject, and, in a feature story quoted them as saying that now after having gone through this they really preferred that the murderer was not found, because they had just been through too much, and this would just revive it all. Is it fitting for those victims of the murderers which capital punishment incites? Without capital punishment they would still be alive. Is it fitting for those executed by mistake? Is it fitting even for the executioner? The most experienced, I might say the "greatest" executioner in modern American-English history published his memoirs in England last year. He very clearly stated that he did not believe capital punishment was a deterrent. Finally, is it fitting for those people who thirst for vengeance, who as Clarence Darrow said "simply love the thought of somebody being killed?" I don't think that that emotion, which perhaps exists to some extent in most of us, should be encouraged or pandered to. I hope I have shown that in order to determine whether or not a law is fitting—or just—you cannot take it abstractly. You have to ask, Is it fitting in the way that it is actually going to work and that history shows that it works? For capital punishment, the answer is no. The second argument is,

Certain hardened criminals are immune to either deterrence or rehabilitation and should receive the ultimate sanction.

Even if this were abstractly so, who is going to pick them? Who is going to decide on those who are beyond rehabilitation? And how? Going back into history, how about Moses? I believe he murdered an Egyptian before he led the Jews into the promised land. What about Paul? If he was not a murderer he was pretty clearly a murderers' helper before God made him an Apostle. To become modern, what about Robert Stroud, a double murderer, who became the "birdman of Alcatraz" and made outstanding contributions to ornithology? How about Nathan Leopold? A prime candidate for the hangman, who later became reformed and, as I recall, made significant contributions to sociology. Or Paul Crump in Chicago, who was described at first as a beast in human form and yet, no one is entirely sure how, with the help of an outstanding warden at the Cook County Jail, he became reformed. And what about the many who receive no publicity? This human experience simply verifies the profound belief, which is implicit in Christianity and other religions, that no human being is totally beyond all hope of reformation.

Thank you for your kind attention.

HOUSE OF REPRESENTATIVES
LANSING, MICHIGAN

27TH DISTRICT
JEFFREY D. PADDEN
LANSING 48909
PHONE: (517) 373-0140

COMMITTEES:
CORRECTIONS (CHAIRPERSON)
CIVIL RIGHTS
SOCIAL SERVICES
URBAN AFFAIRS

Dear Friend:

Recently a movement to reinstate the death penalty was begun in Michigan. Michigan was the first of the 50 states to abolish capital punishment and has been without the death penalty longer than any other government in the English-speaking world. Such a move to reinstate executions needs to be approached cautiously — primarily since it has not proven to be a deterrent to crime.

This booklet, "Why We Should Reject Capital Punishment," has been prepared by Attorney Eugene Wanger, who authored Michigan's constitutional prohibition of the death penalty. It is considered the definitive piece on this issue as it relates to Michigan.

I expect that the potential reinstatement of capital punishment will continue to be a major political and moral issue in the state. I hope the readers will find this booklet useful in sorting through the complex questions that are being raised.

Sincerely,

Jeffrey D. Padden
State Representative

10. Why We Should Reject Capital Punishment

Eugene Wanger

The tendency of civilization to resort to barbarism under stress is a commonplace of history. Thus, frustration over Michigan's serious (although recently reduced) violent crime rate, and wide ignorance of what capital punishment is and what it does, have led many persons to ask if a return to the death penalty for first-degree murder is the answer. That would be quite a step for Michigan, which in 1846 was the first government in the English-speaking world to abolish capital punishment for murder and lesser crimes, and which has never restored it.[1]

In order to examine the question, three vital facts, which are surprising to many, must be understood at the beginning: First, Michigan's penalty for first-degree murder is mandatory life imprisonment, without the right to parole.[2] Only if the Governor exercises his constitutional discretion to commute the sentence is a convicted first-degree murderer even eligible for parole consideration.[3] Second, as the Director of Michigan's Department of Corrections, Perry Johnson, pointed out three years ago, not one convicted first-degree murderer who has been commuted and paroled in Michigan since the parole board was established in 1938 has been returned to prison for committing another murder. Of the 395 who were paroled since 1938, only ten were returned for any reason and five of those were for technical parole violations.[4] The record is similar in other states.[5] Third, taken as a whole, convicted first-degree murderers are the best behaved convicts in prison. Not only in Michigan, but nationally.[6] Perry Johnson, writing four years ago about Michigan's experience, put it this way:[7]

> It is sometimes thought that people serving life sentences will be difficult to manage or control since there is "nothing further that can be done to them." While that may be true in some instances, lifers as a group are actually about the most stable element in any prison population. Some are of great assistance in operating the institution, and normally they do not present serious behavior problems . . .
>
> One argument I have heard for capital punishment is that it is needed to protect the officers in the prison, since the man who has murdered and is serving first-degree life has nothing to fear from murdering again. I can only say that our experience seems to refute this very clearly. We have had but one corrections officer murdered in the history of the Michigan prison system, to my knowledge, as compared with some other states which have capital punishment but which have had many officers murdered by inmates. The one murder of the officer, which occurred last November, was not committed by a man serving first-degree life.
>
> A related point is that lifers, including those serving for first-degree murder, tend to "carry their own weight" to a greater extent than most other prisoners. They are with us long enough to learn important tasks necessary to operation of the institutions, for which we might otherwise have to hire and pay free world employees. Therefore it may well be that the few hundred first-degree lifers in our system actually save the state more than their maintenance cost . . .

This exemplary record is no doubt partly due to Michigan's professionally run corrections system and to the state's long experience in handling convicted first-degree murderers. However, it is not unusual. The record is substantially similar elsewhere.[8]

The Uses of Punishment. So if, as has often been said, the possible uses of punishment are (1) reformation, (2) prevention and (3) retribution, the above facts tell us a good deal: They show that the risk of more killings by convicted first-degree murderers is negligible; and they are more than consistent with the belief, implicit in Christianity and other religions, that no human being is beyond hope of reformation.

Reformation. What about those killers who allegedly "can't be reformed"? Here, too, an answer is clear: There is no way accurately to predict who will become reformed, and no way of knowing with any degree of moral certainty who will not. All we know is that there have been many, many successes, even with the most vicious cases. In short, the hope of reforming even the worst killer is based on experience as well as faith, and capital punishment destroys it. To say that a person's life is "sacred" until it is thought useful to kill him is a contradiction of terms.

Prevention. The subject of prevention includes the prospect of deterring potential murderers, an important issue which has received careful attention over the last four decades. Probably no single subject in criminology has been studied more. Obviously no penalty will deter all murders; and probably any severe penalty will deter many. The key question is, Will the death penalty deter potential murderers better than life imprisonment? There is no credible evidence that it has, even when the risk of execution for murder in America has been relatively high.

Deterrence. If capital punishment deterred better than life imprisonment, it should show up in the homicide rate, for with rare exceptions all homicides in America have been reported since the 1920s. However, forty years of homicide rates show that whether one is a policeman, prison guard or other citizen one is no safer from being a victim of homicide in those states with the death penalty.[9] The abolition of capital punishment in a state does not cause the homicide rate to go up, nor does the restoration of capital punishment or a higher frequency of executions in a state cause the homicide rate to go down.[10] And in those localities where capital punishment is carried out there are no fewer killings near the times of well-publicized executions when any deterrent effect would be greatest.[11] Sometimes there are more.[12] In short, there is no correlation between the ups and downs of the homicide rate, on the one hand, and the presence or absence of the death penalty on the other.

It is like an automobile. If a car runs at the same speed regardless of whether the brakes are on or off, that is pretty strong evidence that the brakes are not working. In the business world, would any reasonable executive adopt a new kind of sales program, for example, in the face of such evidence against it? The logical implication is clear: If would-be murderers consider the consequences at all, they are either deterred as much by life imprisonment as they are by the death penalty or they are planning on not getting caught.

This considerable body of evidence is usually ignored or quickly dismissed by those promoting executions. Their tendency, with some exceptions, as observed by this writer over the past dozen years, has been to argue instead along the following lines:

First, they assert that America's increase in homicide during recent years is a result of the cessation of executions in the late 1960s. Before Gary Gilmore was shot by Utah's firing squad in January, 1977, this country's last execution was in 1967. What they fail to note is that homicide has increased far less than the general crime rate throughout this period. The homicide increase is admittedly serious. But it is plainly irresponsible to suggest that it is attributable to the cessation of executions when, in fact, the rate of increase of crimes that were never punished by death has steadily outstripped the homicide increase by about two-to-one.[13]

Second, they argue that one cannot prove capital punishment does not deter murder because people who are deterred by it do not report the good news to their police departments. The inference they draw is that there are potential Richard Specks and others in our midst, who would be deterred from killing by the death penalty,[14] but would not be deterred by life imprisonment, and that we have no possible way of knowing about them. That is like saying, for example, that we have no way of knowing about traffic safety because motorists do not report in when they are saved from having accidents by traffic safety programs or devices. That, however, has never stopped us from evaluating the effectiveness of those programs and devices by studying their effect on the accident rates where they are used for a reasonable time. Why use a different standard for evaluating the death penalty, especially when we have forty years of homicide rate data to work with?

Third, the advocates of execution refer to a 1973 study by Professor Isaac Ehrlich, the only purportedly empirical study claiming to find any evidence of a deterrent effect of capital punishment. The study is based on a highly sophisticated and arbitrarily designed econometric formula comprising dozens of mathematical components. Its validity, design and findings have been thoroughly discredited by other econometricians at Columbia University,[15] and elsewhere;[16] and, so far as this writer knows, there is not one published econometric analysis (other than Ehrlich's) which supports Ehrlich's result.

Fourth, they allude to statements made to police (almost invariably to the Los Angeles Police Department) by criminal suspects under arrest to the effect that they did not kill or carried a toy gun because they feared the death penalty. The notoriously unreliable character of this anecdotal evidence was well summarized by Professor Anthony Amsterdam in 1972 Congressional testimony as follows:[17]

> Let me point out several things that ought to be said about these reports of what arrested people tell police. First, they assume the police are reporting those conversations reliably. I have my doubts about that. I think the police— like other people—listen and hear very much what they want to hear; and police in most states are for the death penalty . . .
>
> Second, even if the police are being totally level and not misled, the arrested guy will always tell the policeman what he thinks the policeman wants to hear. After conviction, experienced corrections officials like Warden Duffy of San Quentin and Warden Lawes of Sing Sing say the same people tell them, at that point, that they didn't think of the death penalty; and this comes at a time when their stories are more likely reliable because it is too late for what they say to the police to help them.
>
> Number three, the stories about carrying toy guns and what have you ignore the fact that robbers often carry toy guns in Wisconsin and Michigan

and in the other abolitionist states, too. For very good reason: there are lots of people who are robbers but not murderers, and don't want to kill, in the same way that you and I don't want to kill—not because of the death penalty, but because we could not take a life just for money.

And fourth, even if you take these statements of arrested persons at face value, all they show is that a greater penalty deters more. If you had the same people who are arrested in a state where robbery was punishable by fifteen years, and murder was punished by life imprisonment, they would tell you, "We did not kill because we were afraid of life imprisonment." In a state where the penalty for murder is death, they say the same thing by saying, "We were afraid of the electric chair." All that either of these statements is doing is describing what the maximum penalty is that, in fact, the law subjects them to. They are not saying you need capital punishment to frighten these men. They might just as well be frightened by life imprisonment.

And as Dr. LeMoyne Snyder, former medico-legal director of the Michigan State Police and a national homicide authority, pointed out several years ago:[18]

The reason that toy guns are used is because they are cheap; they can be bought in any ten-cent store and usually accomplish their purpose as well as a regular weapon. In states such as Michigan, which abolished capital punishment decades ago, the armed robbery with a toy gun is common.

Fifth, death penalty promoters sometimes list examples of convicted murderers who were not executed, and later killed again. They fail to point out that such cases are extremely rare,[19] that only if the prior murder was first-degree is the case relevant (since no one wants to punish second-degree murder with death)[20] and that in most instances the second killing would not have happened but for lax security precautions or political (rather than professional) prison administration. As pointed out above, the risk of such repeat killings in a well-run penal system is negligible.

Finally, after all this, the response of many advocates of execution is to ask us to "take a chance." All we can possibly lose if we are wrong, they say, are the lives of "vicious and depraved" killers.[21] Even putting humanitarian considerations aside, we have a lot more to lose than that.

Utilitarian Evils. Capital punishment brings with it a number of severe practical evils which we cannot afford. It seriously obstructs the certainty and swiftness of conviction and punishment, which is society's best deterrent to crime. It degrades the administration of justice and distorts the course of the criminal law. It causes the death of innocent persons by inciting additional killings, and by occasionally executing the innocent. It is inflicted discriminatorily against non-whites, severely aggravating racial tensions.

Certainty. Authorities agree that certainty and swiftness of conviction and punishment are the best deterrent to crime. Yet experience shows that juries often refuse to convict where the defendant's life may be at stake, and that where the penalty is life imprisonment, more convictions are possible with less delays. This has happened so often that there is a special name for it: "jury nullification." It has long plagued English and American legal history, and the Louis Harris Poll of June 14, 1973, disclosed that even where guilt was clear, almost one-third of the Americans surveyed were not sure they could vote to convict if the defendant would be executed.[22] These facts take on added significance now that juries can no longer be "death qualified" as they could before *Witherspoon v. Illinois;*[23] and jury verdicts, of course, must be unanimous. Surely it is better that two first-degree murderers be sent to prison for life, than that one be executed and the other freed or convicted of a substantially lesser crime.

This problem is not unknown to the criminal sub-culture. As one professional who worked in group therapy programs in Michigan's prisons for many years put it,[24] "From most of my lifer friends I have heard statements like this: 'If there had been capital punishment in Michigan, I would never have served a day.' To a man, they are aware of the difficulty of getting convictions where the sentence is to be death."

Swiftness. Where the penalty is death the legal proceedings generally take much longer and are more fully fought out at every conceivable point, from selecting the jury to the last desperate motion, collateral attack, clemency hearing and appeal. Not even the most far-fetched possibility can be overlooked. The inevitable publicity invites it and the life at stake demands it. The resulting delay makes the deterrent effect of expeditious conviction and punishment impossible. It also costs much more, and the state must pay the costs of the defense, as well as the prosecution, when the defendant is indigent.[25]

The Administration of Justice. The sensational publicity-potential of capital punishment provides a great political temptation to prosecutors, which experience shows has often degraded the administration of justice. Dr. LeMoyne Snyder, recently writing from California, put it this way:[26]

> One must realize that in many cases there is a deep political motivation involved in the performance of their duties. A lawyer becomes a prosecutor by political process and he requires publicity to become a judge or go to congress or otherwise improve his status. There is little publicity in a murder trial that is started and finished and no longer in the news in a day or two. But there is enormous publicity in murder trials that last for weeks and even months in which the names of the principal parties become household words. Capital punishment is the compelling force that makes this possible. And particularly to get the accused executed is regarded by some prosecutors as an enviable mark of distinction. Let anyone who thinks otherwise read some transcripts of murder trials where the prosecutor is pleading to the jury for the death of an individual sitting only a few feet away and in the vernacular of the courtroom "going for the jugular." Extinguishing a human life appears to become of little consequence and to me the exhibition is revolting.

Another degrading but equally practical use of capital punishment was described by Hans W. Mattick:[27]

> For one thing, the lazy prosecutor whose main interest lies in increasing his conviction rate in the furtherance of his political career finds the mere existence of the death penalty on the statute books to be an exceedingly useful, coercive device for obtaining easy convictions. In the bargaining system of justice that too frequently exists, the lazy prosecutor can always

offer *not* to invoke the death penalty in exchange for a plea of guilty from a defendant who may be difficult to prosecute on the basis of the evidence. Such a coercive use of the death penalty disproportionately exposes the innocent to the possibility of execution for they have no motive to plead guilty. The bargaining power that the mere existence of capital punishment gives to the lazy, but ruthlessly ambitious, prosecutor is the most immoral of reasons for retaining it . . .

If any Michigan reader finds these characterizations startling (and certainly no slur against any Michigan prosecutor is intended), he or she should remember that they are made by professional observers of what actually happens in death penalty states, whereas our state has been without it for 130 years.

The Course of the Law. The death penalty also damages the administration of justice because appellate judges, like juries, sometimes distort the course of the criminal law in their sincere efforts to apply it justly to an appellant whose life is at stake. As Mr. Justice Jackson of the United States Supreme Court candidly admitted, "When the penalty is death, we, like State court judges, are tempted to strain the evidence and even, in close cases, the law in order to give a doubtfully condemned man another chance."[28] James V. Bennett, former director of the Federal Bureau of Prisons, bluntly testified before Congress in 1968 that,[29]

> At bottom, the retention of the death penalty has led to all sorts of controversial not to say inconsistent and erratic decisions of our courts on such things as mental responsibility for crime, use of confessions, admissibility of evidence, arrest and arraignment procedures, and so on.

Such results are in the very nature of things when judges who deeply value human life are immersed in an atmosphere so incompatible with the cool, rational processes of thought that are necessary to the best application and development of the law.

Additional Killings. Capital punishment causes additional killings. These include the so-called "suicide-murder" cases, many of them clinically documented of persons who wanted but feared to take their own lives and committed murder so that the state would execute them.[30] They include imitative killings by the weak minded, who are incited by the sensational publicity of capital trials. A famous example is the Michigan murder by Alfred Hotelling in the wake of the California Hickman trial in the 1920s.[31] No one knows how many murders are indirectly caused by the moral lesson which the death penalty teaches to many: That killing is a permissible, even desirable solution to human problems. As Professors Morris and Hawkins said in their book *The Honest Politician's Guide to Crime Control*,[32]

> If . . . we are to be sincere in our efforts to reduce violence, there is one type of violence that we can with complete certainty eliminate. That is the killing of criminals by the state. The question is, Will people learn to respect life better by threat or by example? And the uniform answer of history, comparative studies and experience is that man is an emulative animal.

Some death penalty advocates respond that executions should increase respect for human life.[33] But the maxim "practice what you preach" is believed by many, and it is difficult to convince them that we should kill people, who kill people, to prove that killing people is wrong. For those to whom examples speak louder than words, capital punishment is often a brutalizing hypocrisy. In short, as George Bernard Shaw put it, murder and capital punishment are not opposites that cancel one another, but similars that breed their kind.[34]

Executing the Innocent. Conviction of the innocent does occur, and execution makes a miscarriage of justice irrevocable. Professor Hugo Bedau in his well-known book, *The Death Penalty in America*, individually documents seventy-four cases since 1893 in which it has been responsibly charged and in most of them proved beyond doubt that persons were wrongfully convicted of criminal homicide in America.[35] Eight of the seventy-four were executed. Edward Radin and others specifically identify many additional cases.[36] Both document how difficult it is to uncover the facts when the authorities do not cooperate.

In Michigan alone since 1910, *at least* twelve persons are known to have been wrongfully convicted of first-degree murder. Later, for most of them years later, they were proved innocent. They are Robert MacGregor, Alexander Ripan, Lloyd Prevost, Vance Hardy, Gerald Crowden, Louis Gross, "Paget," Willie Calloway, Charles Clark, Ephriam Clark, Lindberg Hall and Sceola Kuykendall. The even more recent New Mexico bikers' case, and Florida's Pitts and Lee case, have already become legendary.[37]

How many other innocent men and women have been convicted "beyond a reasonable doubt" of murder, and how many executed? How often have perjured testimony, mistaken eyewitness identification and even (as evidence was produced to show in the case of Louis Gross) a "frame-up" passed for truth? Considering how hard it is to uncover the facts after conviction, let alone after execution, it is obvious that there are more of these miscarriages of justice than we know. Executing a prisoner removes all motive for trying to save his or her life; and creates a host of motives for stifling further investigation: Political careers are at stake, and sometimes serious criminal liability, too, should proof of innocence be found.

Death penalty promoters frequently assert that procedures and safeguards imposed by Supreme Court decisions now make convicting the innocent impossible. It must, therefore, be emphasized that no possible judicial safeguards can prevent convicting the innocent. The known cases were almost invariably caused in one of four ways: (1) Mistaken eyewitness identification, one of the most prevalent dangers of our or any judicial system. (2) Perjured testimony by a convincing liar. (3) A frame-up. (4) The failure by an over-zealous prosecutor to disclose evidence of innocence known to him but not known to the defense. None of these causes are procedural. Further, it is important to remember that in almost all the known cases the defendant was proved not to have been the person who did the actual killing. First-degree murder requires much more than killing; and mistakes by the jury on the defendant's premeditation, sanity or self-defense, being almost always wholly subjective decisions, can rarely if ever be proved. No known "safeguards" can prevent these things. Only if the truth is discovered can the erroneous conviction be reversed. When the defendant has been executed, it is too late.

Discriminatory Infliction. Revival of the death penalty will severely aggravate racial tensions because the rate of execution of blacks in this country far exceeds the proportion of capital crimes committed by black defendants. Of all persons executed in America since 1930, 53.3% have been black although blacks have made up only about ten percent of the population.[38] On June 1, 1977, 51.9% of America's death row population was non-white.[39] The pattern is clear even after conviction and sentencing, even in Northern states. As the Washington Research Project pointed out:[40]

> A study of commutations in Pennsylvania between 1914 and 1948 revealed that whites were nearly twice as likely as blacks to have their sentences commuted. A similar study in New Jersey found almost precisely the same pattern—whites were twice as likely as blacks to have death sentences commuted. In Ohio, over a ten-year period, seventy-eight percent of blacks sentenced to death were actually executed, while only fifty-one percent of whites were.

As stated by Bowers in his recent book, *Executions in America*,[41]

> Studies of death row populations in various states have consistently found that blacks were less likely than whites to have their death sentences commuted. The size of these racial differences in commutations varies from state to state with the largest differences tending to occur in the South. But in virtually every state where meaningful comparisons could be made, the condemned black man had less chance of receiving a commutation than his white counterpart.

As it is with executions, so it is with the sentencing: Of persons who have been convicted of capital crimes, a higher proportion of blacks than of whites have been sentenced to death.[42]

There is much similar evidence, particularly from the Southern states, in which numerous non-racial factors were statistically evaluated to determine if any factor other than race could explain these results. None was found.[43]

Given America's history of slavery and violent prejudice, where as Clarence Darrow said a few decades ago, in some places it was merely "an afternoon's pleasure to kill a Negro,"[44] those findings are not surprising. Despite recent progress toward racial justice in Michigan, it is wishful thinking to assert that discriminatory execution "can't happen here."

Retribution or Vengeance? Since all severe punishment may be seen and felt as retribution, there has been little practical need to ask if there is any difference between retribution and vengeance, which all right-thinking people condemn. If one wants to revive the death penalty <u>as</u> retribution, that question must be asked. This writer submits that there is no difference between retribution and revenge, at least where the death penalty is involved. For the great majority of mankind, who are little given to philosophical distinctions, executions pander to the lust for blood revenge which is present, to a greater or lesser degree, in all of us. The lesson of history is that such pandering is both evil and dangerous; and that the suppression of vengeance remains one of the most arduous and important goals of civilization.

Although these are not the only reasons for opposing the death penalty, the above facts should be more widely known. Were this so there would be fewer cries for capital punishment, and more work for effective law enforcement. Michigan has been without the death penalty longer than any other government in the English-speaking world. It would be a tragedy of international consequence if we restored it.

NOTES

1. *See* A. Post, *Michigan Abolishes Capital Punishment*, 29 MICHIGAN HISTORY MAGAZINE 44–50 (1945); D. Davis, *The Movement to Abolish Capital Punishment in America, 1787–1861*, 63 AM. HIST. REV. 23–46 (1957)
2. MICH. COMP. LAWS §§ 750.316, 791.234 (M.S.A. §§ 28.548, 28.2304)
3. MICH. CONST. art. 5, § 14 (1963); *see* comment of Governor's legal advisor K. Frankland in *Letters on the Penalty of Death*, Michigan Committee Against Capital Punishment (1975) [hereinafter cited as LOPD].
4. Lou Gordon Show, WKBD-TV (Channel 50), Detroit, Mich., Feb. 16, 1974. *See*

also P. Johnson in LOPD.

5. Parole data from seven other states were summarized by the Friends Committee on Legislation in *This Life We Take* (1970), showing that of 994 murderers paroled over a total of 172 years only two were imprisoned a second time for murder. Similarly, the national UNIFORM PAROLE REPORTS NEWSLETTER of Dec., 1972, shows that of the 6,908 persons paroled after conviction for Willful Homicide during the years 1965–1969, 98.23% were successful on parole during the crucial first year after release. They had no new major convictions or allegation of offenses resulting in their return to prison. "Willful Homicide" in this study included all degrees of murder and all types of manslaughter, except negligent manslaughter, manslaughter by vehicle, or negligent homicide.

6. T. SELLIN, THE DEATH PENALTY, The Am. Law Inst. (1959), pp. 69–79

7. LOPD, *op. cit.*

8. SELLIN, *loc. cit.*

9. *See, e.g.,* LAWES, MAN'S JUDGMENT OF DEATH, (1924); SELLIN, *op. cit.*; Schuessler, *The Deterrent Influence of the Death Penalty*, 284 ANNALS 54 (Nov., 1952); SELLIN (ed.), CAPITAL PUNISHMENT, Harper & Row (1967); Savitz, *The Deterrent Effect of Capital Punishment in Philadelphia*, reprinted in Bedau, *infra*, at 315; Graves, *The Deterrent Effect of Capital Punishment in California*, reprinted in Bedau, *infra*, at 322; MATTICK, THE UNEXAMINED DEATH, John Howard Assn. (1966); Forst, *The Deterrent Effect of Capital Punishment, a Cross-State Analysis of the 1960s*, 61 MINN. L. REV. 743 (MAY, 1977); Campion, *Does the Death Penalty Protect State Police*, reprinted in Bedau, *infra*, at 301; Sellin, *Does the Death Penalty Protect Municipal Police*, reprinted in Bedau, *infra*, at 284; Testimony of Thorsten Sellin in Hearings of the Subcommittee on Criminal Laws & Procedures of the U.S. Senate Committee on the Judiciary, 90th Cong., 2d Sess. (1968) pp. 80–83 (hereinafter referred to as *Senate Hearings*).

10. *See, e.g.,* T. SELLIN, THE DEATH PENALTY, *op. cit.*, at pp. 34–38; and articles summarized by W. BOWERS in EXECUTIONS IN AMERICA, Lexington Books (1974) at pp. 18–20.

11. BOWERS, *op. cit.*, at p. 20

12. *idem*

13. Based on the UNIFORM CRIME REPORTS of the F.B.I.; *see, Consolidated Reply Brief for Petitioners*, pp. 4–6 in Jurek v. Texas, 428 U.S. 262 (1976).

14. The *Speck* and *Manson* cases, which seem to be those most often mentioned by execution advocates [for example see F. CARRINGTON, THE VICTIMS, Arlington House (1975) p. 185], are of course outstanding examples of killers who were not deterred by the death penalty.

15. *See* P. Passell & J. Taylor, *The Deterrence Controversy: A Reconsideration of the Time Series Evidence*, in CAPITAL PUNISHMENT IN THE UNITED STATES. AMS Press (1976) pp. 359–371; P. Passell & J. Taylor, *The Deterrent Effect of Capital Punishment: Another View*, reprinted in "Reply Brief for Petitioner" in Fowler v. No. Carolina, 428 U.S. 325 (1976).

16. *See* W. Bowers & G. Pierce, *The Illusion of Deterrence in Isaac Ehrlich's Research on Capital Punishment*, 85 YALE L.J. 187 (1975); Forst, *op. cit.*

17. *Hearings Before Subcommittee No. 3, House Committee on the Judiciary*, 92nd Cong., 2d Sess. (1972) pp. 65–66 on H.R. 8414, 8483, 9486, 3243, 193, 11797 and 12217 (hereinafter referred to as *House Hearings*). The Los Angeles Police Department also supplied the similar anecdotal evidence used in the *Love* case dissent of California Justice Marshall McComb (16 Cal. Reptr. 777 at 785), who more recently has become the only state supreme court justice in American history to have been forced to retire from office because of senility (63 Am. Bar Assn. J. 1470–1471).

18. *This Life We Take, op. cit.,* at p. 17

19. SELLIN, THE DEATH PENALTY, *op. cit.,* p. 72

20. Or do they? F. Carrington included three such cases (in which the first murder was second-degree) in the list of six he described to Congress in *House Hearings, op. cit.,* at pp. 239–240. There would seem to be no logical reason to mention these cases (*Purvis, Gilbert* and *St. Martin*) unless one wanted the death penalty for second-degree (*i.e.,* unpremeditated) murder.

21. *Viz:* F. CARRINGTON, THE VICTIMS, *op. cit.,* at p. 188; E. VAN DEN HAAG, PUNISHING CRIMINALS, Basic Books (1975), at p. 216. Or they often argue that the death penalty is justified if its deterrent effect saves "one life," as did F. Carrington in *House Hearings, op. cit.,* at p. 223, apparently

ignoring the innocent lives which are taken as a result of capital punishment.

22. *The Harris Survey*, Thursday, June 14, 1973

23. 391 U.S. 510 (1968), holding that jury membership in capital cases could no longer be strictly limited to persons who support the death penalty.

24. Prof. Jack Schwartz, Dept. of Social Science, Lansing Community College, in LOPD, *op. cit.*

25. Washington Research Project, *The Case Against Capital Punishment*, Wash., D.C. (1971) pp. 61–62

26. LOPD, *op. cit.*

27. MATTICK, *op. cit.*, at 39–40

28. Stein v. New York, 346 U.S. 156, 196 (1953)

29. *Senate Hearings, op. cit.*, at 35

30. See SELLIN, THE DEATH PENALTY, *op. cit.*, at 65–69; West, *Medicine and Capital Punishment, Senate Hearings, op. cit.*, at 124–129; Testimony of Bernard Diamond, M.D., to the Calif. Senate Committee on Governmental Efficiency, April 12, 1967; and articles by West, Solomon and Diamond in 45 AM. J. OF ORTHOPSYCHIATRY. NO. 4 (JULY, 1975).

31. BREARLY, HOMICIDE IN THE UNITED STATES, Univ. of N.C. Press (1932) p. 38

32. Univ. of Chicago Press (1970) p. 76

33. *Viz:* E. VAN DEN HAAG, *op. cit.*, at 213

34. Quoted by A. Multner, M.C., in Rept. #677 of the U.S. House Committee on the Dist. of Columbia, 87th Cong., 1st Sess. (1961).

35. H. BEDAU (ed.), THE DEATH PENALTY IN AMERICA, Revised Edn., Anchor Books (1967) pp. 440–452

36. E. RADIN, THE INNOCENTS, Wm. Morrow & Co. (1964); McNamara, *Convicting the Innocent*, 15 CRIME & DELINQUENCY 57 (1969), and works there cited; MATTICK, *op. cit.*, at 35–36

37. The Detroit News, Jan. 22, 1975, p. 1A; "The Inside Story of How The News Freed 4 From Death Row," Detroit News SUNDAY MAGAZINE, Jan. 11, 1976; G. MILLER, INVITATION To A LYNCHING, Doubleday (1975); Miami Herald, Sept. 19, 1975; Daily News, Sept. 19, 1975.

38. Federal Bureau of Prisons, NATIONAL PRISONER STATISTICS, No. 46

(Aug., 1971) p. 1

39. Based on information provided by the NAACP Legal Defense Fund, ACLU affiliates, and official sources, as reported by the Nat'l. Coalition Against the Death Penalty.

40. Washington Research Project, *op. cit.*, at p. 52

41. BOWERS, *op. cit.*, at p. 74

42. CAPITAL PUNISHMENT IN THE UNITED STATES, *op. cit.*, at 105

43. *idem,* at 108 *et seq.*

44. "Is Capital Punishment a Wise Policy?" debate at the Metropolitan Opera House, New York City, Sept. 23, 1924, reprinted in MACKEY (ed.), VOICES AGAINST DEATH, Burt Franklin & Co. (1976) at p. 169

EUGENE G. WANGER is an attorney practicing in Lansing and is a member of the State Bar of Michigan. He is Co-Chairman of the Michigan Committee Against Capital Punishment. Mr. Wanger authored Michigan's constitutional prohibition of the death penalty.

Originally published by Citizens Research Council of Michigan.

11. Why Michigan Republicans Should Oppose the Death Penalty

Dear Fellow Republican:

Capital punishment—the ultimate government interference with the lives of its citizens—has been outlawed in Michigan for 133 years. This policy was continued as a Republican proposal in our state's present constitution—after careful study and debate in the Republican controlled Constitutional Convention—where it was adopted with only 3 dissenting votes.

In today's emotional atmosphere, it is more important than ever that reason must control emotion in solving our state's problems. Calmly considered, the known facts about the death penalty show:

1. Today in Michigan, the risk of convicted first degree murderers committing more murders is *negligible*.
2. The death penalty fails to deter murder *better* than life imprisonment.
3. The death penalty incites *additional* killings; and occasionally executes the innocent.

4. The death penalty severely *impairs* the certainty and swiftness of conviction and punishment, which is society's best deterrent to crime.
5. The death penalty violates the religious teaching—which is supported by wide experience—that *no* human being (even one who must be kept behind bars for life) is beyond hope of reformation.

These and other aspects of the question are detailed in the attached material.
Sincerely,

Lansing   Eugene G. Wanger, Co-Chrm.
August 1980   Michigan Committee Against Capital Punishment

12. Capital Punishment and Law Enforcement

Guest Columnist:

(EDITOR'S NOTE: Sydney Harris, writing recently in his syndicated article, remarked, "The paradox of punishment is that even the threat of it is effective against those who least need it, whilst the most severe infliction of it is futile against those who most merit it." At the invitation of LACHES, Lansing attorney Eugene G. Wanger has prepared the following article on the subject of capital punishment. Attorney Wanger is co-chairman, along with Tom Downs, of the Michigan Committee Against Capital Punishment, of 1202 Michigan National Tower, Lansing, Michigan 48933. He was the author of the prohibition of the death penalty in the 1963 Michigan Constitution. Your comments to this article will be appreciated by Mr. Wanger and by Laches.)

It is probably natural under a representative government that our serious crime problem produce cries for a return of the death penalty. What is unnatural, in the view of this writer, is that these cries should be promoted in the form of proposals without regard for the facts: Facts which show capital punishment to be a severe barrier to effective law enforcement and harmful to society.

A case in point is the recent statement of a Michigan legislator that "People are fed up with first-degree murderers being released to kill again before they have served even a minimum sentence." This statement was widely reported by the press last month. In fact, as the Director of Michigan's Department of Corrections publicly pointed out in February, 1974, not one convicted first-degree murderer who has been paroled in Michigan since the parole board was established in 1938 has been returned to prison for committing another murder. Of the 395 who were paroled since 1938, only 10 were returned for any reason and 5 of those were for technical parole violations. In Michigan first-degree murderers can only be paroled if their life sentence is commuted by the governor.

Additional well-documented evidence shows many of the death penalty's inherent defects: It fails to deter murder. It severely obstructs that certainty and swiftness of conviction and punishment which is society's best deterrent to crime. It distorts the administration of justice and the course of the criminal law. It causes the death of innocent persons, by occasionally executing the innocent and by inciting additional killings by the mentally disturbed. It is inflicted discriminatorily against blacks, severely aggravating racial tensions. And it is immensely expensive.

Forty years of studies fail to show that the death penalty is superior to life imprisonment as a deterrent. They show with remarkable unanimity that whether you are a policeman, prison guard or other citizen you are no safer from being a victim of homicide where they have the death penalty. The abolition of capital punishment in a state does not cause the homicide rate to go up, nor does the restoration of capital punishment or the frequency or executions in a state cause the homicide rate to go down. In short, there is no correlation between the ups and downs of the homicide rate, on the one hand, and the presence or absence of the death penalty, on the other.

It's like an automobile. If your car runs at the same speed regardless of whether the brakes are on or off, that's pretty strong evidence that the brakes are not working. The logical implication is clear: If would-be murderers consider the consequences at all, they are either deterred as much by life imprisonment as they are by the death penalty or they are planning on not getting caught.

Experience also shows that juries often refuse to convict where the defendant's life may be at stake, and that where the penalty is life imprisonment more convictions are possible with less delays. This phenomenon of "jury nullification" has long aggravated English and American legal history; and the Louis Harris Poll of June 14, 1973, disclosed that even where guilt was clear, almost one-third of the Americans surveyed were not sure they could vote to convict if the defendant would be executed. It is far better that two murderers be sent to prison than one to be executed and the other go free.

In addition to impairing the certainty of conviction, capital punishment impairs its speed. Where the penalty is death the proceedings generally take much longer and are more fully fought out at every conceivable point—from selecting the jury to the last desperate appeal. Not even the most remote possibility can be overlooked. The inevitable publicity invites it and the stakes demand it. The resulting delay makes the deterrent effect of expeditious conviction and punishment impossible. It also costs much more, and the state must usually pay the costs of the defense, as well as the prosecution, because the defendant is indigent.

The sensational publicity-potential of capital punishment provides a great political temptation to prosecutors, which experience shows has often degraded the administration of justice.

Dr. LeMoyne Snyder, national homicide authority and former Medico-Legal Director of the Michigan State Police, recently writing from California put it this way:

> One must realize that in many cases there is a deep political motivation involved in the performance of their duties. A lawyer becomes a prosecutor by political process and he requires publicity to become a judge or go to congress or otherwise improve his status. There is little publicity in a murder trial that is started and finished and no longer in the news in a day or two. But there is enormous publicity in murder trials that last for weeks and even

months in which the names of the principal parties become household words. Capital punishment is the compelling force that makes this possible. And particularly to get the accused executed is regarded by some prosecutors as an enviable mark of distinction. Let anyone who thinks otherwise read some transcripts of murder trials where the prosecutor is pleading to the jury for the death of an individual sitting only a few feet away and in the vernacular of the courtroom "going for the jugular," Extinguishing a human life appears to become of little consequence and to me the exhibition is revolting.

The death penalty also damages the administration of justice because appellate judges sometimes distort the course of the law itself in their sincere efforts to apply it justly to an appellant whose life is at stake. As Mr. Justice Jackson candidly admitted, "When the penalty is death, we, like State court judges, are tempted to strain the evidence and even, in close cases, the law in order to give a doubtfully condemned man another chance." James V. Bennett, former Director of the Federal Bureau of Prisons, bluntly testified in 1968 that,

> At bottom, the retention of the death penalty has led to all sorts of contro-versial not to say inconsistent and erratic decisions of our courts on such things as mental responsibility for crime, use of confessions, admissibility of evidence, arrest and arraignment procedures, and so on.

Such results are in the very nature of things when judges who deeply value human life are immersed in an atmosphere so incompatible with the cool, rational processes of thought that are necessary for the best application and development of the law.

Conviction of the innocent does occur, and execution makes a miscarriage of justice irrevocable. Professor Hugo Bedau in his well-known book *The Death Penalty in America* individually documents 74 cases since 1893 in which it has been responsibly charged and in most of them proved beyond doubt that persons were wrongfully convicted of criminal homicide in America. Eight of the 74 were executed. Edward Radin and others specifically identify many additional cases. Both document how difficult it is to uncover the facts when the authorities do not cooperate.

In Michigan alone since 1910, at least 12 persons are known to have been wrongfully convicted of murder. Later, for most of them years later, they were proved innocent. They are Robert MacGregor, Alexander Ripan, Lloyd Prevost, Vance Hardy, Gerald Crowden, Louis Gross, "Pagent," Willie Colloway, Charles Clark, Ephriam Clark, Lindberg Hall and Sceola Kuykendall.

How many other innocent men and women have been convicted "beyond a reasonable doubt" of murder, and how many executed? How often have perjured testimony, mistaken eyewitness identification and even (as evidence was produced to show in the case of Louis Gross) a "frame-up" passed for truth? Considering how hard it is to uncover the facts after conviction, let alone after execution, it is obvious that there are more of these miscarriages of justice than we know.

Thomas Jefferson said, "I shall ask for the abolition of the punishment of death until I have the infallibility of human judgment presented to me." Has Michigan demonstrated that infallibility?

Capital punishment causes additional murders. These include the so-called "suicide-murder" cases, many of them clinically documented of persons who wanted but feared to take their own lives and committed murder so that the state would execute them. They include imitative killings by the weak minded, who are incited by the sensational publicity of capital trials. A famous example is the Michigan murder by Alfred Hotelling in the wake of the California Hickman trial in the '20s. No one knows how many murders are indirectly caused by the moral lesson which the death penalty teaches to many: That killing is a permissible, even desirable solution to human problems. As Professors Morris and Hawkins said in their book *The Honest Politician's Guide to Crime Control*,

> If . . . we are to be sincere in our efforts to reduce violence, there is one type of
> violence that we can with complete certainty eliminate. That is the killing of
> criminals by the state. The question is, Will people learn to respect life better

by threat or by example? And the uniform answer of history, comparative studies and experience is that man is an emulative animal.

As Bernard Shaw put it, "Murder and capital punishment are not opposites that cancel one another, but similars that breed their kind."

Revival of the death penalty in practice will severely aggravate racial tensions because the rate of execution of blacks in this country far exceeds the proportion of capital crimes committed by black defendants. Of all persons executed in America since 1930, 53.3 percent have been black although blacks have made up only about ten percent of the population. Leaving aside the experience of the south, consider the evidence from the north where, as the Washington Research Project pointed out, the pattern is clear even after conviction and sentencing:

> A study of commutations in Pennsylvania between 1914 and 1948 revealed that whites were nearly twice as likely as blacks to have their sentences commuted. A similar study in New Jersey found almost precisely the same pattern—whites were twice as likely as blacks to have death sentences commuted. In Ohio, over a ten-year period, 78 percent of blacks sentenced to death were actually executed, while only 51 percent of whites were.

Despite recent progress toward racial justice in America, it is wishful thinking to assert that "It can't happen again."

Finally—and surprising as it may be to many advocates of execution—life imprisonment is financially much cheaper than the death penalty, saving public revenue urgently needed to effectively fight crime. The Director of Michigan's Department of Corrections pointed out in March, 1974, that the prisoners then serving time in Michigan for first-degree murder, when you averaged them out, were financially carrying their own weight. This should not be surprising, for as the internationally respected criminologist Thorsten Sellin stated in 1959, "In a well-organized penal system, murderers as a group can undoubtedly earn their keep."

On the other hand, both the litigation and the prison costs are greatly increased where there is capital punishment. The greater length of death penalty proceedings has been considered above. The extra cost of it all, including judge and lawyer time, courtroom space, security arrangements, stenographer costs and printing briefs and records can run very high. The Sirhan and Manson murder trials alone are said to have cost the state of California close to a million dollars.

Examining only the prison costs of capital punishment, Richard McGee, administrator of the California correctional system, stated:

> The actual costs of execution, the cost of operating the super-maximum security condemned unit, the years spent by some inmates in condemned status, and a pro-rata share of top level prison officials' time spent in administering the unit add up to a cost substantially greater than the cost to retain them in prison for the rest of their lives.

Although these are not the only reasons for opposing the death penalty, the above facts should be more widely known among the bench and bar—and the citizenry—of the state. Were this so there would be fewer cries for capital punishment, and more work for effective law enforcement. Michigan has been without the death penalty longer than any other government in the English-speaking world. It would be a tragedy of international consequence if we restored it.

Pontiac-Oakland County Legal News, September 26, 1975.

Courtesy of:
Michigan Committee Against Capital Punishment
524 South Walnut Street, Lansing 48933

13. Point of View—Eye for Eye No Aid

James H. Brickley

In the last few years we have been witnessing in this state and country a groundswell for the reestablishment of capital punishment. There have been attempts, and I am sure there will be others, in the State Legislature to have us return to the death penalty for the first time since 1846.

I believe the movement results from shock, outrage and repulsion at some vicious incomprehensible crimes which a dazed citizenry is seeking to stop.

THE PUBLIC is puzzled. It is puzzled at the development of this condemnable violence and frustrated as to what can be done about it.

This confusion and uncertainty, along with justified anger, has led to a degree of emotionalism.

The mood of our people is understandable. The daily headlines detailing cold-blooded murders of policemen, U.S. diplomats and the frightening airline hijacking have created psychological shockwaves.

UNFORTUNATELY, AN emotion-laden atmosphere does not permit sober reflection.

The recommendation for the death penalty emanates from excited public opinion which has blinded us to the real issues involved. In my opinion, it would be a giant step backward in the legal, moral and humanitarian development of our society, as well as for effective law enforcement, if this movement to reestablish capital punishment succeeds.

Our system of criminal justice needs improvement, to be sure. But, I do not believe reenactment of the death penalty is improvement. In my view, it would be very regrettable to permit the pendulum to swing back to a period in criminal justice history which is pockmarked with crude and ineffective measures.

THE MOST prevalent and frequent premise offered for the reestablishment of capital punishment is that it would deter crime. On the surface it would appear that even the hardened criminal fears nothing more than death. Thus, it is argued, if capital punishment were a real danger, it would deter the commission of some of the recent abhorrent crimes.

The deterrence premise does not withstand close examination. There simply is no empirical data which would even suggest the death penalty has helped to effectively stem crime. But there are facts and statistics indicating it is no deterrent whatsoever.

As research has revealed so clearly, murder generally is a crime of passion, committed in an emotional state where the consequences of the act are rarely considered. Capital punishment would have little deterrent value.

THERE IS much we do not know about human behavior. Our lack of sophistication in this field causes us to fall back on our emotions in frustration over attempts to protect ourselves. Despite some ignorance, behavioral scientists do agree—and all of the facts in law enforcement seem to bear them out—that punishment is irrelevant in deterring crimes of compulsion and passion.

In terms of preventing criminals from repeating their offenses, it must be observed that those who would be targets of capital punishment—murderers primarily—generally are the best prisoners and have the lowest recidivism rate.

One research study states: "Murderers are the least likely of all classes of offenders to return to crime when they are paroled or released. They make the best prisoners." If deterrence can be discounted, then what is the basis for this recent demand for the reinstitution of the death penalty?

I BELIEVE the recent wave of unconscionable violence has awakened the natural human instinct for vengeance. This is quite understandable.

The nation has been so outraged and shocked at the unbelievable and abhorrent crimes it has recoiled with the demand for revenge.

I would hope, however, that tempers and emotions cool to permit an objective analysis of the problem. I would hope we, as a nation, have outgrown the "eye for an eye" theory. I would hope we learn something from our past. While the axiom states that "history repeats itself," I do not believe it must be inevitable that we repeat our previous mistakes.

OUR HISTORY books are replete with details of the barbarity practiced by government in the name of protecting society. We need no new chapters.

When we resort to this erroneous logic, society itself is guilty of irrationality by not considering the validity of its actions. The net result is, I am afraid, that we engage in emotional arguments while ignoring the crucial issue: How can we give ourselves the ultimate degree of protection?

The public is entitled to protection. It is no secret society is dissatisfied with the job that has been done in this regard. It is entitled to more protection than has been provided. I would suggest if we dealt with crime more decisively, and in some cases more stringently, there would be less public frustration.

I WOULD suggest that abuse of parole and probation has been one of the factors which has led to demands for capital punishment. For instance, the knowledge that in one jurisdiction 63 per cent of those who were convicted of a second felony were placed on probation, leads to justified public outrage.

In discussing sentencing practices, I think we often overlook our primary obligation to protect society.

I stress this point because we should not fall victim to the argument of being too "soft" or too "tough" in sentencing. If we are going to have a stable and fair criminal justice system, we must not only oppose the unnecessary death penalty but we must also be honest enough to recognize the need for more realistic sentencing to give the public the protection to which it is entitled.

WE HAVE acted too often during a wave of passion only to regret the decisions made in periods of high emotion. I hope we will not add to our list of regrets.

LT. GOV. BRICKLEY, who lives on a farm near Dimondale, is a former Detroit City Councilman, Wayne County chief assistant prosecutor, U.S. attorney for Eastern Michigan and FBI agent. He is chairman of the Michigan Crime Commission.

Reprinted from the *Lansing State Journal.*

Courtesy of National Council on Crime & Delinquency in Michigan.

14. Meeting of the Representative Assembly of the State Bar of Michigan: Excerpts

Proceedings had by the Representative Assembly of the State Bar of Michigan at Room 3037, Upper Level, Cobo Hall, Detroit, Michigan, on Thursday, September 23, 1982, at the hour of 10:00 a.m.

APPEARANCES:

DAVID A. GOLDMAN, Chairperson
RICHARD D. REED, Clerk
HON. GENE SCHNELZ, Parliamentarian
MICHAEL FRANCK, Executive Director

MR. GOLDMAN: The motion carries.

We are now back to Item No. 12, the special order of business, consideration of a proposed amendment to the Michigan Constitution eliminating the prohibition against the death penalty.

The proposal is that there be an amendment to the Michigan Constitution eliminating the prohibition against the death penalty.

I will call upon Mr. Eugene G. Wanger at this time, a Lansing attorney who I understand was the author of the original prohibition that has now found its way into the Constitution of the State of Michigan. Mr. Wanger.

MR. WANGER: Mr. Chairperson, ladies and gentlemen of the Bar: The tendency of civilization is to resort to barbarism under stress is a commonplace of history. Thus, frustration over Michigan's serious violent crime rate, and wide ignorance of what capital punishment is and what it does, has caused many persons to ask if we should restore the death penalty for first-degree murder as an answer.

That would be quite a step for Michigan, which by statute in 1846 was the first government in the entire English-speaking world to abolish the death penalty for murder and lesser crimes, and which has never restored it.

Today, those advocating this punishment, which has now been abandoned by most of the Western world, except America and South Africa, often say that it will deter murder and serve justice.

On deterrence, the key question is whether it will deter murders or potential murders better than life imprisonment. There is no credible evidence that it has, even when the risk or execution for murder in America was relatively high.

If capital punishment deterred murder better than life imprisonment, it should show up in the homicide rate, for with rare exceptions, all homicides in America have been reported since the 1920's.

However, 40 years of homicide rates show that whether one is a policeman, prison guard, or other citizen, one is no safer from being a victim of homicide where they have the death penalty. The abolition of capital punishment in the state does not cause the homicide rate to go up, nor does the restoration of capital punishment or higher frequency of executions there cause the homicide rate to go down.

And in those localities where capital punishment is regularly carried out, there are no fewer killings near the time of well-publicized executions when any deterrent effect would be greatest.

In short, there is no correlation between the ups and downs of the homicide rate, on the one hand, and the presence or the absence of the death penalty on the other.

It is much like your automobile. If your car runs at the same speed regardless of whether the brakes are on or off, that is pretty good evidence that the brakes are not working.

This considerable body of published research I have referred to—and there is a great deal of it—is usually ignored or quickly dismissed by those promoting executions. Their tendency, with some exceptions, as observed by me over the past dozen years, has been argued more along the following lines:

They quote the United States Supreme Court *Gregg* opinions. While a majority, as you know, of the Court in that case held capital punishment legal, they never held it good.

Although the Court's legal pronouncements are always entitled to respect, their views of sociological phenomena—hardly their specialty—may, without disrespect be taken for what they are worth.

The previous speaker didn't emphasize, I believe, or tell you that the opinion which he quoted—which, by the way, was the opinion of only three of the Justices—to the effect that capital punishment deters, he did not reflect the fact that when they addressed the key question on the same or adjoining page of their decision, the key question of whether it deterred murder better than life imprisonment, even those three Justices found that the answer on the basis of the evidence they had was inconclusive.

Indeed, no one has ever denied that the death penalty deters. Of course it deters as compared with nothing. The key question which we must all keep in our minds is: Does it deter better than life imprisonment?

The advocates of execution also refer to a study by Isaac Ehrlich. The study is based upon a highly sophisticated and arbitrarily designed econometric formula comprising dozens and dozens of mathematical components.

Its validity, design and findings have been thoroughly discredited by other econometricians at Columbia University, and elsewhere, and there is only one other published econometric analysis, which has equally been discredited, I might add, that supports Ehrlich's result.

Now, here's what Professor Laurence Klein, recipient of the 1980 Nobel

Prize in Economics, President of the American Economic Association, had to say in his careful study of Ehrlich's work, which was commissioned, by the way, by the National Academy of Sciences: " . . . it seems unthinkable to us to base decisions on the use of the death penalty on Ehrlich's findings . . ." His findings are so "weak" that they "could be regarded as evidence of a counterdeterrent effect of capital punishment."

Capital punishment brings with it a number of severe practical evils which we cannot afford. It seriously obstructs the certainty and swiftness of conviction and punishment, which is society's best deterrent to crime.

It causes the death of innocent people by inciting additional killings, and by occasionally executing the innocent. It is inflicted discriminatorily against non-whites, severely aggravating racial tensions.

Authorities agree that certainty and swiftness of conviction and punishment are the best deterrent to crime. The experience shows that juries sometimes refuse to convict where the defendant's life may be at stake, and that where the penalty is life imprisonment, more convictions are possible with less delays.

This jury nullification has long been a phenomena of English and American legal history. And the Louis Harris Poll of June 14, 1973, disclosed that even where guilt was clear, almost one-third of the Americans surveyed were not sure they could vote to convict if the defendant would be executed.

While bifurcated trials can mitigate the effect of jury nullification, there is nothing in the realm of procedural reform that can eliminate it when the penalty is death.

And when the penalty is death, the legal proceedings generally take much longer, and are much more fully fought out at every conceivable point. Not even the most farfetched possibility can be overlooked, as you might well imagine. The inevitable publicity invites it, and the life at stake demands it.

The resulting delay makes the deterrent effect of expeditious conviction and punishment impossible. It also costs much more, and the state must pay the costs, usually of the defense, as well as the prosecution, when the defendant is indigent.

As Wayne County Prosecutor and strong death penalty foe, William

Cahalan, said here in Detroit at a press conference this Monday: "I would not hesitate to say that every capital case would cost the taxpayers at least a half a million dollars." This is money that could otherwise be used to effectively fight and prevent crime.

Indeed, in terms of actual tax dollars, all you can be sure of saving by executing a few prisoners each year is the cost of their food and laundry. This is far exceeded by the extra judicial costs and extra prison costs of having the death penalty.

Capital punishment causes additional killing. These include the so-called "suicide-murder" cases, many of them clinically documented, of persons who wanted but feared to take their own lives and committed murder so that the state would execute them.

Babysitter Pamela Watkins, after unsuccessfully trying to commit suicide, smothered her young charges to death so that the state would execute her; just one example. Recent evidence suggests that Gary Gilmore may have been another one.

These cases include imitative killings by the weak minded who are incited by the sensational publicity of capital trials. A famous example is the Michigan murder by Alfred Hotelling in the Bay City area in the 1920's, in the wake of the California Hickman trial.

No one knows how many murders are indirectly caused by the moral lesson which the death penalty teaches to many, which is that killing is a permissible, even desirable, solution to human problems. As Professors Morris and Hawkins said in their book, *The Honest Politician's Guide to Crime Control*: "If . . . we are to be sincere in our efforts to reduce violence, there is one type of violence that we can with complete certainty eliminate. That is the killing of criminals by the state. The question is, Will people learn to respect life better by threat or by example? And the uniform answer of history, comparative studies and experience is that man is an emulative animal."

Conviction of the innocent occurs, and execution makes a miscarriage of justice irrevocable. Professor Hugo Bedau in his well-known book, *The Death Penalty in America*, documents individually 74 cases since 1893 in which it has been responsibly charged, and in most cases proved, without doubt, that persons were wrongfully convicted of criminal homicide in America. Eight of them were executed. Both he and others document how difficult it is to uncover the facts after an execution.

In Michigan, since 1910, at least 12 persons are known to have been convicted of first-degree murder. Later, for most of them many years later, they were proved innocent.

I hold in my hands clippings from the recent press in the country, which just happened to come to me in my search for this material, some in Michigan, some elsewhere, of over a dozen persons in the same category during the last two years, all post-Furman, all recent, that show that our system is not capable of avoiding mistakes.

And if we look at the real majority opinion in the *Gregg* case itself, the one that was signed by five Justices, we find this language: "Imposition of the death penalty is surely an awesome responsibility for any system of justice and those who participate in it. Mistakes will be made and discrimination will occur which will be difficult to explain."

On the subject of discrimination, this only needs to be said: Studies in state after state show that a Black person who has been convicted of a capital crime is more likely to be sentenced to death—and if sentenced, more likely to be executed—than a white person convicted of that crime.

Last year the Michigan Department of Corrections examined the data in Oakland County and reported in this document, which Mr. Patterson, I believe, is aware of, that Blacks—or rather that Black defendants—were more likely than white defendants to be convicted of first-degree murder there. Despite progress towards racial justice in Michigan, it is wishful thinking to believe that discriminatory execution can't happen here.

In conclusion, despite all of this, our state's current death penalty spokespersons contend that justice demands the death penalty. It is hard to tell exactly what sort of justice they have in mind, since their recent ballot petition goes far beyond Michigan's statutory definition of first-degree murder, and would make the death penalty available for accidental killings as well.

Twenty-one years ago our state's Constitutional Convention of 144 delegates, dominated by Republicans—many of them very conservative—and containing six distinguished retired Circuit Judges, voted to prohibit capital punishment. Most of them were experienced people. They knew how vicious crime could be. One had been shot and nearly killed on the floor of the U.S. Congress.

Yet the proposal to prohibit capital punishment passed overwhelmingly, with only three dissenting votes. Was their sense of justice deficient? I don't think so.

What has changed since then? Certainly the number of violent crimes, and the public anger over them, has increased.

I share that anger after a brutal slaying—and I have only a half-minute left—and understand how many people could feel that such a killer should die.

But I would ask them, is it worth satisfying that sense of justice to have a penalty that will inevitably cause the death of additional innocent persons; is it worth satisfying that feeling to have a penalty that makes law enforcement more difficult and even more costly; is it worth satisfying it to have a system that will often execute a man or woman, not because they are a murderer, but because they are Black?

And finally, I would ask them to consider that it is implicit in Christianity, and other religions, that no human being is beyond hope of reformation.

I conclude, as I hope you will conclude, that the abolition of capital punishment was, and is, a significant contribution to the cause and concept of civilized justice, which all of us seek to serve. Thank you.

MR. GOLDMAN: Thank you, Mr. Wanger.

Ladies and gentlemen of the Assembly, I think that we have had an outstanding presentation. . . .

15. Michigan Committee Against Capital Punishment History

524 South Walnut Street
Lansing, Michigan 48933

The Michigan Committee Against Capital Punishment (MCACP) was organized in 1972 to oppose efforts to restore the death penalty in Michigan. Our state, by statute in 1846, was the first government in the English-speaking world to abolish capital punishment for murder and lesser crimes. It has never restored it.

In 1964 Michigan abolition achieved constitutional status when the voters accepted a new state constitution providing "No law shall be enacted providing for the penalty of death." (Article IV, Section 46)

Over the years the MCACP has actively participated—on the hustings, through the news media and in state and federal court—in defeating five different state-wide petition drives seeking to repeal Michigan's constitutional death penalty ban. It engages in research, education, publication and advocacy; and has access to perhaps the largest private collection of death penalty literature in America. In the late 1970s it was co-organizer, with the Michigan ACLU, of the Michigan Coalition Against the Death Penalty; and it has participated in every annual conference of the National Coalition to Abolish the Death Penalty since its inception.

The MCACP is co-chaired by Eugene G. Wanger, who is the author of Michigan's constitutional prohibition of capital punishment, and Tom Downs, who was Vice-president of the state's Constitutional Convention and is one of America's leading practitioners in the field of election law.

Its numerous publications include Letters on the Penalty of Death (1975), Why We Should Reject Capital Punishment (1978) and Death Penalty Arguments & Updates (1990).

The MCACP may be reached at the above address or by telephoning area code 517, number 484-9497.

10/91

16. The Penalty of Death—What It Does to the Living

William Kime and Eugene Wanger, Esq.

[This thought provoking article presents a public policy perspective and offers arguments which may be used in testimony or discussion. It was written for the Michigan Coalition Against the Death Penalty. The Michigan Catholic Conference, a member of the coalition, is pleased to reproduce it here in its entirety.]

Historically, the debate over the merits of capital punishment has been waged primarily on two fronts, its ethical justification and its efficacy as a deterrent of capital crimes. While many advocates of the death penalty now concede that the case for deterrence lacks support, they continue to argue that some particularly heinous crimes demand nothing less than death as an adequate sanction. Given the strong and sincere feelings on both sides of the issue this debate over morality may never be resolved.

As the Michigan Legislature has been invited once again to consider adoption of the death penalty, a review of other states where some 190 executions have taken place over the last sixteen years suggests that other areas of difference must also be placed in the balance. The purpose of this brief review is to help insure that those who must make this difficult decision do so only after review of evidence from states with actual experience in the administration of the penalty of death.

THE IMPACT OF CAPITAL PUNISHMENT IN OTHER JURISDICTIONS

Nothing in current experience restores the widely discredited argument that executions deter capital crime against either citizens in general or law enforcement and corrections personnel. What is evident, however, is that the death penalty has brought the states which have it serious problems with cost and the efficiency of their criminal justice system operations. It is also clear that the risk of executing the innocent remains unabated.

COST

Some still argue for the death penalty on the basis that the public should not bear the burden of maintaining convicted murderers in prison for life. But execution is not the answer, for the death penalty carries a much higher price tag than life imprisonment.

In the first place, capital cases must be treated much differently than ordinary prosecutions and trials to maintain compliance with Supreme Court rulings. In practice, they take more than three times as long to conclude. They involve extensive pre-trial motions, elaborate background investigations, and numerous expert witnesses whose considerable fees on both sides of the case are typically funded by the taxpayer. In addition, attorneys' fees are much higher in capital cases and a separate, perhaps longer, trial must be held after conviction to determine the sentence. Then review at the State Supreme Court level is mandatory, and there are likely to be several levels of appeal and/or retrials. That this costly procedure *always* takes years may be fortunate in view of the cases—more than one—in which enough time elapsed for the exoneration of innocent persons before execution.

Compare this process (the cost of which ranges from at least $600,000 to more than $2 million) with the typical criminal case, which is settled by a guilty plea rather than a trial and the reasons for the cost and time differences are obvious.

The cost of housing death row inmates is also a major factor. Staff-intensive, super-secure facilities cost much more to run than general population prisons in which "lifers" are housed. In fact, death-row costs alone can be greater than the cost of maintaining a prisoner for life.

To illustrate that costs are real and unavoidable, we cite the following excerpts from *Millions Misspent*, an October 1992 report by the Death Penalty Information Center.

- In Texas, a death penalty case costs taxpayers an average of $2.3 million, . . . about three times the cost of imprisoning someone in a single cell at the highest security level for forty years. In Florida, each execution is costing the state $3.2 million. The New York Department of Correctional Services estimated that implementing the death penalty would cost the state about $118 million *annually*.
- In Florida, a mid-year budget cut of $45 million for the Department of Corrections forced the early release of 3,000 inmates. Yet by 1988, Florida had spent $57.2 million to accomplish the execution of 18 people. It costs six times more to execute a person in Florida than to incarcerate a prisoner for life with no parole.

As costly as capital punishment is to the state, it is local governments who are hit the hardest. They pay for the trials and retrials. Here are some additional examples from *Millions Misspent*:

Even where the state provides some of the money for the counties to pursue the death penalty, the burden on the county can be crushing. California, for example, was spending $10 million a year reimbursing counties for expert witnesses, investigators and other death-penalty costs, plus $2 million more to help pay for the overall cost of murder trials in smaller counties. But . . .

In Sierra County, California authorities had to cut police services in 1988 to pick up the tab of pursuing death penalty prosecutions. The County's

District Attorney, James Reichle, complained, "If we didn't have to pay $500,000 a pop for Sacramento's murders I'd have an investigator, the sheriff and a couple of extra deputies and we could do some lasting good for Sierra County law enforcement. The sewage system at the courthouse is failing, a bridge collapsed, there's no county library, no county park." The county's auditor, Don Hemphill, said that if death penalty expenses kept piling up, the county would soon be broke. Hemphill indicated that another death penalty case would likely require the county to lay off 10 percent of its police and sheriff force.

In Imperial County, California, the county supervisors refused to pay the bill for the defense of a man facing the death penalty because the case would bankrupt the county. The County Budget Officer spent three days in jail for refusing to pay the bill.

In Lincoln County, Georgia, county commissioners also refused to pay the defense costs (for retrial of a death row inmate). . . . The commissioners were sent to jail. Walker Norman, chair of the County Commission, explained: "We're a rural county of 7,500 people with a small tax base. We had to raise taxes once already for this case when it was originally tried, and now we are going to have to raise taxes again. It's not fair."

In Yazoo City, Mississippi, the town is worried that they, too, might get stuck with an expensive death penalty case. "A capital murder trial is the worst financial nightmare any government body could envision," said the editor of the local paper.

Norman Kinne, Dallas County (Texas) District Attorney, expressed his frustration at the expense. ". . . though I'm a firm believer in the death penalty, I also understand what the cost is. . . . if you can be satisfied with putting a person in the penitentiary for the rest of his life . . . I think maybe we have to be satisfied with that as opposed to spending $1 million to try and get them executed . . . I think we could use (the money) better for additional penitentiary space, rehabilitation, education (and) especially devote a lot of attention to juveniles."

BURDEN ON THE CRIMINAL JUSTICE SYSTEM

The examples cited above demonstrate how the death penalty soaks up money needed for other public services, including law enforcement. But money is not the only issue here, time is also a limited resource. Our circuit and appellate courts are tied up and backlogged now; more lengthy trials and more reviews would exacerbate that problem beyond measure. *Millions Misspent* informs us that:

> Some state appeals courts are overwhelmed with death penalty cases. The California Supreme Court, for example, spends more than half its time reviewing death cases. The Florida Supreme Court also spends about half its time on death penalty cases. Many governors spend a significant percentage of their time reviewing clemency petitions. As John Dixson, Chief Justice (retired) of the Louisiana Supreme Court, said, "The people have a constitutional right to the death penalty and we'll do our best to make it work rationally. But you can see what it's doing. Capital punishment is destroying the system."

IRREVERSIBLE ERROR: THE EXECUTION OF THE INNOCENT

Supporters of the death penalty claim that, while it has happened in the past, procedural and appellate safeguards now make it a virtual impossibility for an innocent person to be put to death by the state. The truth is that the risk remains little diminished by such measures. An examination of some 350 past cases[1] shows why this is true:

In the first place, few wrongful convictions result from the kind of procedural errors most likely to be flushed out on appeal or retrial. The most common source of error is perjured testimony, often supplied by witnesses in exchange for leniency in their own proceedings. In a few cases the murder victim turned up alive and in many others there were mistaken eye-witness identifications. It is not surprising that such errors are commonly brought to light by sources outside the formal process of appeal or retrial.

Also, the fact that the trial is a capital one introduces its own biases; a natural reaction to the media attention is to "go for the jugular." And since no person opposed to the death penalty may serve on the jury, it does not represent an unbiased sample of the community. Studies have shown that such a jury is more likely to rule for conviction.

That wrongful sentences of death must still sometimes occur is no matter of conjecture. In March of this year a man who for six years sat on Alabama's death row was found wrongfully convicted on the basis of perjured testimony. Had recent cut backs in the right to review been in place earlier, it is likely that his restored innocence would have been posthumous. Nothing brings a justice system or entire government into worse repute than the execution of the innocent.

A BETTER ALTERNATIVE: PROVIDING RELIEF FOR THE FAMILIES OF VICTIMS

There is no reason why persons who must spend the remainder of their lives in prison should do so as dead-weight burdens on society. Instead they should be required to work productively to provide some fiscal support to the families of their victims. No punishment, neither a life sentence nor a death sentence, can restore or compensate for a life taken. But the victim's right to restitution is explicitly set out in Michigan's Constitution, and what can be done should be.

At present, while the victims of many lesser crimes receive restitution from convicted criminals, the families of murder victims receive none. Why is that? Because convicted murderers go to prison, and Michigan's Correctional Industries Act (MCLA 800.331) prohibits use of prisoner earnings for any purpose but the prisoner's own welfare and reimbursement to the state. This can be changed. Not only should murderers be required to work productively to reimburse the state for their own maintenance, but they should also be required to provide financial relief to the families of their bereaved victims.

No constitutional change is needed to accomplish this, only amendments to existing statutes. We feel that as a direction for legislative action, this should take precedence over a gesture which can do nothing for victims, except victimize them further when the tax bills come due.

CONCLUSION

Experience is said to be the best teacher—perhaps because it is the costliest. In this matter, fortunately, Michigan can, if it will, benefit from others' experience. Experience which makes it clear that whatever our moral, ethical, and religious persuasions on this matter, the implementation of capital punishment—a public policy wisely rejected by Michigan for more than 145 years—would impose a crushing burden on the legal and criminal justice systems of state and local government to the detriment of other duties, including the prosecution of other serious criminal cases.

In short, while the death penalty may appeal to some as a means of being, or seeming, "tough on murderers," actual practice—not hope or opinion or belief, but hard evidence—proves it to cost much and accomplish little or nothing. Cities in states like Texas, where executions are carried out more often than anywhere else, continue to show higher murder rates than many cities like New York, where capital punishment is not an option. There are about a thousand murders a year reported in Michigan; execution of a handful of people a year, more than is likely, would hardly serve as a deterrent, and would do nothing about the current prison population which numbers more than thirty-five thousand.

For all these reasons, and because of the risk of executing the innocent, we recommend continuation of life imprisonment without parole, but with restitution added, as an avenue for legislative action which puts the real needs of victims' families ahead of hollow vengeance at high public cost.

NOTE

1. Bedau and Radelet, Miscarriages of Justice in Potentially Capital Cases, 40 Stanford Law Review, 21, 1987.

WILLIAM KIME is an independent corrections consultant and former Deputy Director, Michigan Department of Corrections. EUGENE WANGER, ESQ. is the author of Michigan's constitutional prohibition of the death penalty and Co-Chairman of the Michigan Committee Against Capital Punishment.

Michigan Catholic Conference *FOCUS*, vol. 21, no. 2 April 1993.

17. Michigan Senate Judiciary Committee Hearing on the Death Penalty

Oakland Community College

September 8, 1994

TESTIMONY OF EUGENE G. WANGER

My name is Eugene G. Wanger. I am co-chairman, with Tom Downs, of the Michigan Committee Against Capital Punishment. I am the author of our state's Constitutional prohibition of the death penalty.

Michigan, by statute in 1846, was the first government in the English-speaking world to abolish capital punishment for murder and lesser crimes. Our state has never restored it. Since 1964 our state Constitution has prohibited it. It would be a tragedy of international consequence to restore it now.

Thirty years ago the Michigan Constitutional Convention passed that death penalty prohibition with only three dissenting votes, calling this step ". . . a significant contribution to the concept of civilized justice, which all of us seek to serve."

What has changed since then? Certainly not the facts about what the death penalty is and what it does. Mountains of evidence show that the nature of the death penalty remains the same.

Nothing in current experience restores the widely discredited argument that executions deter capital crimes against either citizens in general or against law enforcement and corrections personnel. What is evident, however, is that the death penalty has brought the states which have it serious problems with cost and the efficiency of their law enforcement operations. It is also clear that the risk of executing the innocent remains unabated.

Cost. It is now widely recognized that the death penalty carries a much higher price tag than life imprisonment. This is because capital cases must be treated much differently than ordinary prosecutions and trials to comply with Supreme Court rulings. In practice, they take more than three times as long to conclude. They involve extensive pre-trial motions, elaborate background investigations, and numerous expert witnesses whose considerable fees on both sides of the case are usually funded by the taxpayer. In addition, attorney fees are much higher in capital cases and a separate, often longer, trial must be held after conviction to determine the sentence. Then review at the state Supreme Court level is mandatory, and there are likely to be several levels of appeal and retrial. That this costly process always takes years may be fortunate, in view of the cases in which enough time elapsed for the exoneration of innocent persons before they were executed.

In addition, the housing of death row inmates is a major cost factor. Staff-intensive, super-secure facilities cost much more to build and run than general population prisons in which most "lifers" are housed. In fact, death row costs alone can be greater than the expense of maintaining a prisoner for life.

The total dollar cost of this process is staggering, ranging from at least $600,000.00 to more than $2 million per case. The following facts are cited from *Millions Misspent,* an October 1992 report by the Death Penalty Information Center in Washington:

- In Texas, a death penalty case costs taxpayers an average of $2.3 million, . . . about three times the cost of imprisoning someone in a single cell at the highest security level for 40 years. In Florida, each execution is costing the state $3.2 million. The New York Department of Correctional Services estimated that implementing the death penalty would cost the state about $118 million annually.
- In Florida, a mid-year budget cut of $45 million for the Department of Corrections forced the early release of 3,000 inmates. Yet by 1988 Florida had spent $57.2 million to accomplish the execution of 18 people. It costs six times more to execute a person in Florida than to incarcerate a prisoner for life with no parole.

As costly as capital punishment is for the state, it is local governments who are hit the hardest because they pay for the trials and retrials.

- County Commissioners in Sierra and Imperial Counties, California, and Lincoln County, Georgia, were sent to jail because they couldn't—or wouldn't—pay these staggering additional costs. And essential services had to be cut.
- The District Attorney of Dallas County, Texas, although a believer in the death penalty, expressed his frustration over its cost by saying ". . . I think we could use [the money] better for additional penitentiary space, rehabilitation, education [and] especially devote a lot of attention to juveniles."

Error. The mounting evidence also shows that the risk of occasionally executing the innocent is substantial. An examination of over 350 cases of mistaken conviction (collected by Professors Bedau and Radelet) shows why. Few of them result from the kind of procedural errors most likely to be flushed out on appeal or retrial. The most common cause is perjured testimony, often supplied by jail witnesses in exchange for leniency in their own proceedings. In a few cases the murder victims even turned up alive; and in many others there was mistaken eye-witness identification. Such errors are commonly brought to light by sources outside the formal criminal justice process . . . by pure good luck.

Also, the death penalty process is biased in favor of conviction. This is based on a natural reaction to the media attention to "go for the jugular." And since no person who is opposed to the death penalty can sit on the jury, it does not represent an unbiased sample of the community and studies have shown that such juries are more likely to convict. All this makes error more likely.

<u>A Better Alternative</u>. There is no reason why persons who must spend the rest of their lives in prison should do so as dead-weight burdens on society. Instead they should be required to work productively to provide some financial support to the families of their victims. No punishment can restore or compensate for a life taken. But the victim's right to restitution is now explicitly set out in our Constitution, and what can be done should be. However, Michigan's Correctional Industries Act (MCLA 800.331) prohibits this restitution. I urge you to repeal that statutory restriction. This should take precedence over capital punishment which can do nothing for victims, except victimize their families further when the tax bills come due.

Experience is said to be the best teacher—perhaps because it is the costliest. In this matter, fortunately, Michigan can, if it will, benefit from others' experience. Experience which makes it clear that whatever our ethical or religious persuasions on this matter, the restoration of capital punishment—a policy wisely rejected by Michigan for more than 145 years—would impose a crushing cost burden on the legal and criminal justice systems of state and local government to the detriment of other duties, including the prosecution of other serious criminal cases.

In short, while the death penalty may appeal to some as a means of being, or seeming, "tough on murderers," actual practice—not hope or opinion or belief—proves it to cost much and accomplish little or nothing. Cities in states like Texas, where executions are carried out more often than anywhere else, continue to show higher murder rates than many cities like New York, where capital punishment is not an option. There are about a thousand murders a year reported in Michigan; execution of a handful of people a year, more than is likely, would hardly serve as a deterrent, and would do nothing about the current prison population which numbers more than thirty-five thousand.

For all these reasons, and because of the risk of executing the innocent, I recommend continuation of life imprisonment without parole, but with restitution added, as an avenue for legislative action which puts the real needs of victims' families ahead of hollow vengeance at high public cost.

18. What Prosecutors Won't Tell You

Speaking against the death penalty, America's most distinguished prosecuting attorney, in the *New York Times* for February 7, 1995, emphasized "the dirty little secret" that the death penalty "actually hinders the fight against crime." This kind of statement was immensely helpful when it appeared, since at the time very few prosecutors were willing to speak out against capital punishment.

Mr. Morgenthau eloquently described the immense sums of money squandered in maintaining the practice, one that fuels the flames of violence and intimidates many politically fearful prosecutors from publicly opposing it.

He stated that the data from more than one hundred years "has not produced credible evidence that executions deter crime." Instead, the certainty and swiftness of conviction and punishment, and focusing on recidivists and career criminals, is the answer. And the evidence from Manhattan confirms this, he explained. Moreover, a 1989 study estimated that the death penalty would cost New York $118 million a year.

Manhattan's District Attorney concluded his extraordinary article by describing how the innocent are sometimes sent to death row and the "brutalizing and dehumanizing effect" capital punishment has upon society.

[The use here of this abstract instead of including the original article, is explained in the preface.]

Robert M. Morgenthau, "What Prosecutors Won't Tell You,"
New York Times, February 7, 1995.

19. Michigan House Committee on Judiciary and Civil Rights: Hearing on the Death Penalty

State Capitol Building
July 13, 1995

TESTIMONY OF EUGENE G. WANGER

My name is Eugene G. Wanger. Since 1973 I have been Co-chairman, with Tom Downs, of the Michigan Committee Against Capital Punishment. As a Delegate to our State's 1961 Constitutional Convention, I authored Michigan's Constitutional prohibition of the death penalty. I am a past national board member of the National Coalition to Abolish the Death Penalty and my collection of material on the subject perhaps is the largest in the Country in private hands.

I am here to urge you to vote against capital punishment; and in particular to vote against House Joint Resolution "N," which would attempt to apply that penalty to the sensational crimes of multiple murder and terrorism.

Michigan, by statute in 1846, was the first government in the English-speaking world to abolish capital punishment for murder and lesser crimes.

Our state has never restored it. Beginning in 1964, Article IV, Section 46, of our state Constitution prohibits it. Today almost every Western industrialized nation has abandoned it; and the principal executing nations are now China, Iraq, Iran, Nigeria and—sadly—the United States.

Thirty-four years ago the 144 Delegates to Michigan's Constitutional Convention—two-thirds of them Republican, most of them very conservative and six of them retired Circuit Court Judges who had presided over some of the blackest and bloodiest murder trials in American history—passed this death penalty prohibition with only three dissenting votes. They called this step ". . . a significant contribution to the concept of civilized justice, which all of us seek to serve."

What has changed since then? Certainly not the facts about what the death penalty is and what it does. Mountains of evidence show that the nature of the death penalty remains the same.

There is still no credible evidence that it deters murder any better than life imprisonment. The homicide rates still fail to show that you are any safer from being a victim of homicide where they have the death penalty . . . and that is so whether you are a policeman, prison guard or ordinary citizen. Probably no single subject in criminology has been studied more.

It is still inflicted arbitrarily and capriciously, often on the basis of race and poverty . . . and on those who have the less able lawyers.

It still causes additional killings by the weak-minded who seek suicide by execution, by the mentally ill who see themselves as society's executioner, by fanatics seeking martyrdom and by those who are brutalized by capital punishment.

And it still costs immense additional sums of money and seriously impairs the certainty and swiftness of conviction and punishment which is society's best deterrent to crime.

But the worst things the death penalty does, in my view, are that it snuffs out the lives of additional innocent people and it makes the terrible situation of the murder victim's families even harder. Society may (or may not) have a duty to see that criminals get what they deserve, but it has a much stronger duty to protect the innocent.

For capital punishment has and will continue to occasionally execute the innocent, for reasons which no procedural or appellate safeguards can prevent. Mounting evidence shows this risk is substantial. An examination of over 350 cases of mistaken conviction for capital crimes (collected by Professors Bedau and Radelet) shows why. The most common cause is perjured testimony, often supplied by jail prisoners in exchange for leniency in their own cases. Sometimes there was a deliberate frame-up. In a few cases the murder victims even turned up alive; and in many others there was honestly mistaken eye-witness identification. Hardly a month goes by without a new case being discovered. Most often the error is brought to light outside the formal criminal justice process . . . by pure good luck. That so many only escaped by luck indicates that many more of these innocents didn't escape at all.

House Joint Resolution "N" only makes this risk of error worse because the sensational trials are where the risk of error is greatest. The heat is on for results and political hay can be made—and lawyers even go to Congress—if a conviction is obtained. And providing capital punishment for terrorism will only make Michigan families desirable targets for fanatical terrorists seeking martyrdom.

Moreover, the death penalty is often repugnant to the victim's family. Even where it is not, the lengthy death penalty process often greatly prolongs their grief and makes any restitution to them by the killer impossible.

Instead murderers should be required to work in prison to provide some financial support to the families of their victims. No punishment can restore or compensate for a life taken. But since 1988 the victim's "right to restitution" has been explicitly set out in Article I, Section 24(1), of our state Constitution, and what can be done should be. However, Section 11(1)(b) of Michigan's Correctional Industries Act (MCLA 800.331) prohibits this restitution. If you care for victim's families, I urge you to repeal that statutory restriction. So far, not one Bill has been introduced to do it. This should take precedence over capital punishment which can do nothing for victims, except victimize their families further.

And I beg those families who think they can only be satisfied by the execution of the killer to accept a little bit less, so that other innocent lives can be saved.

Experience is said to be the best teacher—perhaps because it is the costliest. In this matter, fortunately, Michigan can, if it will, benefit from others' experience. Experience which makes it clear that the restoration of capital punishment—a policy wisely rejected by Michigan for 149 years—would be a financial and moral tragedy.

In short, while the death penalty may appeal to some as a means of being, or seeming to be, "tough on murderers," actual practice—not hope or opinion or belief—proves it to cost much and accomplish little or nothing . . . except add to the pile of bodies. I urge you to vote against this Joint Resolution and for the continuation of life without parole, but with restitution added, as a course of legislative action which puts the real needs of victims' families ahead of hollow vengeance at high public cost.

20. Michigan Committee Against Capital Punishment

Co-Chairmen: Tom Downs and Eugene G. Wanger
October 6, 1997
Honorable Ted Wallace, Chair House Committee on the Judiciary Michigan
    State Capitol—Room 375
Lansing, Michigan 48933

      Re: Hearing of October 7th on HJR "M" (Death Penalty)

Dear Representative Wallace:

    Being prevented by a prior commitment from attending this hearing, I would like to present the enclosed testimony in opposition to HJR "M", which would authorize the death penalty in our historic abolition state for those who murder a corrections officer.

    Virtually all of the evils of capital punishment generally apply with equal vigor to this particular proposal. However, there are two aspects of the social science research which should be specially noted.

First, the evidence fails to show that prison guards or police personnel are any safer from being victims of homicide where they have the death penalty.

Second, some people commit murder because they want the state to execute them. There are clinically documented cases of this. Usually the perpetrators are mentally ill or very stressed, not unlike many in our prisons. For them capital punishment is more like a reward. For these gentry, HJR "M" will make Michigan corrections officers into targets for murder.

Respectfully,
Eugene G. Wanger

Encl.: Testimony

Michigan House Committee on the Judiciary
Hearing on HJR "M" (Death Penalty)
Michigan State Capitol
October 7, 1997

TESTIMONY OF EUGENE G. WANGER ON THE EVIDENCE AGAINST THE DEATH PENALTY

In 1787, when the American patriot Dr. Benjamin Rush of Philadelphia began the movement to abolish the death penalty in our country, there was very little in the way of what we would call "scientific evidence" bearing on the subject. Instead, Rush and his early followers relied mostly on a clear faith in the efficacy of human reason stemming from the 18th Century European Enlightenment (including the arguments advanced by the Italian Cesare Beccaria in his famous 1764 essay "On Crimes and Punishments"); on a strong belief in the hopeful message of the Gospels (Rush himself was a staunch Christian); and upon a widely shared feeling born of the American Revolution that, since harsh and bloody laws marked monarchies, mild and benevolent ones should characterize republics.

It was not that Rush lacked an understanding of the scientific method. He had earned his medical degree at the University of Edinburgh in Scotland (which was probably the finest University in the English-speaking world at that time) before returning to sign the Declaration of Independence and serve in the Revolution. The problem was rather that then (and for many decades afterwards) there was almost nothing available in the way of reliable criminal statistics.

DETERRENCE

The first evidentiary matter to attract the attention of Rush's contemporaries was the question of what effect the repeal of capital punishment—which was then a punishment for scores of different crimes in Europe, as many as 200 in England and about a dozen in early America—would have on the commission of crimes. The official reports from abroad indicated that the repeal or restriction of the death penalty by those few European monarchs who had done so had not led to an increase in murder and mayhem but, to the contrary, was in some cases followed by a reduction. The anecdotal experience also failed to show that executions discouraged crime, as in England where picking pockets was a hanging offense—and where the London pickpockets most successfully plied their trade at public executions when everyone else "was looking up." Moreover, English juries often refused to convict the guilty where the penalty might be death; and London's bankers at one point had to petition Parliament to repeal that penalty for forgery so that the crime could be successfully prosecuted. If capital punishment could not visibly deter petty theft and other crimes where the principal motive was simple greed, these abolitionists asked, how could it deter a crime like murder where the passions were so deeply involved?

When Michigan abolished the death penalty for murder and lesser crimes in 1846 (the first government in the English-speaking world to do so), and a few other states followed, their officials frequently were asked if this action had caused the murder rate to go up. Their responses, as shown by the literature of the time, were uniformly negative. The response to this evidence from those who favored the death penalty, as shown by their writings in the 19th Century, was to almost universally ignore it. Mankind was governed by fear, they believed, and it feared nothing so much as it feared death. How then could capital punishment fail to be a deterrent?

As America advanced into the 20th Century, more complete and accurate crime statistics were collected and published which made possible further comparisons bearing on the deterrent effect of capital punishment. As the data accumulated, these comparisons were set out in four groundbreaking and influential books: Raymond Bye's doctoral thesis, *Capital Punishment in the United States* (1919), Warden Lewis Lawes's largely statistical *Man's Judgement of Death* (1924), Englishman Roy Calvert's eloquent *Capital Punishment in the Twentieth Century* (1927), and Criminologist Thorsten Sellin's powerful monograph for the American Law Institute, *The Death Penalty* (1959). Sellin's work, being based on more recent and complete data, is still of great interest today.

These works, along with numerous later scholarly studies, all clearly failed to show that people—whether they are policemen, prison guards or just ordinary citizens—are any safer from being victims of homicide where they have the death penalty. The abolition of that penalty in a state does not cause the homicide rate to go up, nor does its restoration or a higher frequency of executions in a state cause the homicide rate to go down. And in those localities where executions are carried out, there are no fewer killings near the times of well-publicized executions when any deterrent effect should be greatest. Sometimes there are more. In short, there is no correlation between the ups and downs of the homicide rate on the one hand, and the presence or absence of the death penalty on the other. It's like an automobile. If your car runs at the same speed regardless of whether the brakes are on or off, that's pretty strong evidence that the brakes are not working. The evidence was massive, and remarkable for its consistency of agreement. Probably no single subject in criminology had been studied more. The best deterrent, criminologists agreed, was the certainty and swiftness of conviction and punishment, not the draconian severity of the punishment itself.

A shadow was briefly cast on all this social science research in the early

1970s when a practitioner of the abstruse science of econometrics, Professor Isaac Ehrlich, announced that his calculations indicated that every execution "may" lead to several less homicides. Econometrics, unlike more traditional social science analysis, tries to account for many factual variables at a time, instead of just one or two, and requires creating long mathematical formulas of many elements which often have to be based on a good number of arbitrary assumptions. These many elements are all strung together and a very small mistake in one element can produce very large changes in other elements and in the end result. Ehrlich's study, and papers by a few of his disciples, being contrary to all previous research, riveted the attention of the academic community. The National Academy of Sciences commissioned a special study headed by one of the world's leading econometricians, Nobel Laureate and President of the American Economics Association, Professor Laurence Klein, which after careful analysis thoroughly discredited Ehrlich's result. Other scholarly studies agreed. In fairness it should be added that Ehrlich was not a promoter of the death penalty and that his work had been vigorously exploited and exaggerated by many who were promoting it far beyond anything that he had apparently anticipated.

INNOCENCE

Not one unit of government in America keeps a list of its mistakes. It is human nature to deny them, cover them up, or push them into the background as soon as possible. In a few short years the public forgets and the surviving players can breathe more easily. Exceptions exist, but they are few. So it is not surprising that although many references to the execution of the innocent have been made since the beginning of the abolition movement, the surviving evidence of the individual cases has become scattered and hard to find.

As a result of prodigious research efforts, Professor Hugo Bedau in his book *The Death Penalty in America* (1964) and in his Stanford Law Review article written with Professor Michael Radelet, "Miscarriages of Justice in Potentially Capital Cases" (1987), collected 350 examples of mistaken conviction occurring in America since 1900. The decade with the second highest number was the 1970s. All 350 were convicted of the capital or potentially capital crime of murder or rape. Well over half were convicted of first-degree murder. But in all 350 cases it was later discovered either that no crime had been committed (for example, seven of the murder victims turned up alive!) or that the person convicted of the crime was neither physically nor legally involved in it at all. In 88% of these 350 cases, the State itself corrected the error; but in only about 10% did the authors find that the error was discovered by state officials! Usually it was a random stroke of luck that the evidence of innocence was found. But 40% of them had been sentenced to death and 23 had been executed. Later the authors, together with writer Constance Putnam, uncovered and reported 66 more such cases in *In Spite of Innocence* (1992), and today hardly a month seems to go by without another one being reported by the nation's press. How does this happen? Mostly it is perjured testimony or mistaken eyewitness identification. And unhappily it all too often involves inefficiency or corruption in our American legal system, where a very small number of bad actors can do a lot of harm. When you understand how easily these errors can happen and how hard it is to uncover them later, it is obvious that there are far more of these tragic cases than we will ever know.

COST

Many people are astonished when they first hear that the death penalty system costs far more than the life imprisonment system. After all, they say, think of the mouths we won't have to feed. A lot of them seem to feel about life imprisonment for murder like many people felt about the Vietnam War. They don't want their tax dollars to help pay for it. But the truth is about all you can be sure to really save by executing someone is the marginal cost of his or her food and laundry; for the persons executed are such a small part of the whole prison that their absence has no effect on prison programs or staffing or maintenance or even—politics being what they are—on prison building programs.

By taking out a few inmates you can never save their average costs, determined by dividing total prison costs by the total prison population;

and anyone who has ever run a large organization knows this. America now has a death row population of 3,153, which is only 0.27% of our total prison population of 1,164,356. We now execute about 50 of them a year and the number's rising. Even if we executed 500 a year for 30 years that would only add up to 1.29% of the total prison population, assuming it stays about the same. (If it goes up the percentage would be even smaller.) It would be a very rare case indeed where we could save more than the marginal cost with numbers anything like that.

Even if we could save the full average cost of a murderer's life imprisonment by executing him, the evidence shows that the costs of maintaining the state's capital punishment system are far greater. The trials are far longer, the investigations far more involved, the appeals far more complex and the death row costs heavy. Usually the taxpayers must pay for the defense as well as for the prosecution, because the defendant is indigent. A Duke University study, "The Costs of Processing Murder Cases in North Carolina" (1993) estimated that these extra death penalty expenses were costing that state over $2 million per execution. Earlier studies indicated that these extra costs totaled $90 million in California and would total $118 million in New York annually. Texas taxpayers pay an average of $2.3 million per death penalty case, which is about three times the cost of life imprisonment for 40 years there. In Florida the ratio is six times. Without capital punishment, all this money could be used to lower taxes or to fund more effective ways to fight and prevent crime or for some other useful purpose.

It also surprises many people a lot to learn that first-degree murderers, as a whole, are the best behaved group of inmates in prison. The truth, contrary to the political hype, is that those with really tough prison behavior problems are a small percentage. The others, including many who could have been executed, often hold prison jobs in which they save the state considerable money and (where state law provides for it) must pay restitution money from their prison earnings to their victims' families. These cost savings and restitution benefits are cancelled when the culprit is executed.

FAIRNESS

Until perhaps fifty years ago, we Americans had a powerfully strong belief in the value of "fair play." While cultural changes have since rather eroded that belief, there are still many Americans who feel that when big benefits or big burdens are being handed out by the government, it should be done as fairly as possible. The death penalty is the largest burden anyone could receive, and it doesn't even begin to pass the fairness test.

Suppose your prosecutor charges you with murder and wants you executed. The first thing you'd want is a good lawyer to investigate and present your claim of innocence in the best possible light; and even more important if you are found guilty, to show that your guilt is not so black that you should die.

If you've plenty of money . . . Hey! No Problem! The people who get to death row are all (with rare exceptions) dirt poor, so you almost certainly won't qualify. In fact, Warden Clinton Duffy of San Quentin, who presided over 90 executions, called capital punishment "the privilege of the poor." You'll have to pay a fortune in legal fees, but that money won't be wasted.

However, if you're poor, the recent evidence shows you're in deep trouble. The odds are good that (depending on where you live) the judge will assign a grossly underpaid and inexperienced private lawyer to represent you, who may or may not be the best that the judge can find; or you will be assigned to an overworked public defender whose caseload is so huge that he or she can't possibly spare the time to represent you adequately. And very likely neither lawyer will be given enough money for the factual investigation you're desperately going to need.

We are talking about major incompetence here: lawyers who have never tried a criminal case, who don't look up the law, who do nothing to prepare, who never interview the key witnesses, who are asleep or drunk or even absent during part of the trial. Often they are selected through the local political patronage system; and sometimes their principal role seems to be just to speed the trial along. An investigation in Kentucky showed that one-quarter of those under sentence of death there had been represented at trial by lawyers who had since been disbarred or had resigned rather than face disbarment.

If this sounds like a crisis situation, it is. The American Bar Association has been blowing the whistle for years, but almost no one has been listening. Meanwhile the Congress has just drastically cut back the funding for lawyers for indigent death row defendants and the Supreme Court, in a series of cases, and with Congress's help, has been severely cutting back your right to appeal. Once your lawyer makes mistakes in your case, there is often no way to get the errors corrected; and now there are even fewer ways to try. Of course, you can pay for this with your life.

The second thing you're going to want is an impartial jury. One that will decide the case fairly or (let's be frank) that will maybe lean just a little bit in your favor. One that, even if they find you guilty, might just let you live. You're in real trouble here too, because the law requires that in death penalty cases juries have to be "death qualified." That means that no one who is really against capital punishment (and a lot of Americans are) can serve on the jury, which you can understand because without that we'd almost never get anybody executed. The difficulty is that the social science research shows these "death qualified" juries generally are not impartial. They are conviction prone, and much more likely than average to agree with the prosecutor and think that you wouldn't be there in the first place unless you were guilty as charged. There is probably no good way around this. It is a price of unfairness we must pay if we're going to have the death penalty. How do you think you'd like it in your trial?

Third, you will want a judge who really knows the law and will give you all the rights you are entitled to when being tried for your life. It is the glory of our system that even the worst felons are nevertheless entitled to be convicted only in strict accordance with the law. But death penalty law is a specialty. It is very complex and the evidence seems to be that America's state judges, on average, are not very good at it. The president of the American Bar Association has reported that serious constitutional error was found in one-third to one-half of all the state death penalty cases by the federal courts; and since virtually every state death sentence is appealed to federal court, that is a sobering figure. Scholars later reported that death row inmates secured federal court relief in about 47% of their habeas corpus cases between 1976 and 1991. We must hope that this does not really represent an average lack of legal ability in the state courts; but it is clear that there are a lot of state judges who are not applying the law correctly. It's been suggested that instead of following the law, some of these judges are following the election returns, as many voters want executions. Since you won't have any say in who your judge will be . . . Here's Luck!

Fourth, you'll want to be sure that the race of the parties involved won't affect the result of your trial. I know it's annoying to be reminded of race all the time. And if you (like most of us) are white, you're home free anyway . . . Right? Well, not exactly.

Professor David Baldus in *Equal Justice and the Death Penalty* (1990), the most thorough study of the subject ever done, discovered that in Georgia white murder defendants in the city are more likely to be sentenced to death than black murderers are. It's an outrage, but people there seem to be getting the death penalty because they are white! On the other hand, in the rural areas of the state blacks are more likely than whites to be sent to death row, Baldus found. That's monstrous, considering the other race problems blacks have.

Happily, when Baldus put all these figures together for his state-wide study, they cancelled each other out, so that for Georgia as a whole such discrimination doesn't appear in the end result. It reminds one of what the old lawyer said at his retirement party: "When I was young I lost many cases I should have won. When I was old I won many cases I should have lost. And so, in the end, justice was done." If you're a white being tried in the city or a black being tried in the Georgia countryside, perhaps you'll take comfort from that.

When Baldus looked at recent but less detailed studies in some other states, he was unable to determine that discrimination based on the defendant's race existed there, although all the experienced death penalty defense lawyers he talked to were sure that it did. So while it's just possible that this discrimination is unique to Georgia, don't bet on it. You'll have to take your chances. However, the major finding of Baldus's study was not about the race of the defendants. It was about the race of the murder victims. He discovered that, regardless of whether you are a white or a black murderer, in most cases you are much more likely to be sentenced to death if your victim is white—on average, more than four times as likely! Studies from other states strongly agree. In other words, in America death sentences are being handed out on the basis of a factor (the victim's race) which has no bearing on the heinousness of the murder or the moral guilt of the offender. People who are killing whites are getting sentenced to death, and people who are killing blacks are not.

To those Americans who were under the illusion that American law or practice was limiting the death penalty to only the most heinous crimes, this finding was a real eye-opener. It was further confirmation of the highly arbitrary and capricious way in which that penalty is actually inflicted. We read and hear a lot about the sensationally horrible murderers in a state who get the death penalty; but are often completely uninformed about the equally culpable ones there who do not get it and the substantially less culpable ones who do, notwithstanding formal guidelines in all the death penalty states designed to prevent that result.

Warren McCleskey had a particular reason for not liking all this. He was a black man on Georgia's death row for murdering a white person, and he asked the United States Supreme Court for relief on the basis of the Baldus study. While the Court was very nice to Dr. Baldus, it didn't give Mr. McCleskey any help. Even though the study shows a big pattern of race discrimination in death sentencing in your state, the Court said, it doesn't clearly prove that this race discrimination actually happened in your case, so you should take this matter up with the Legislature. (Yes, the Supreme Court actually said that.) Mr. McCleskey, having no swat with the Legislature, is no longer with us. The Supreme Court is full of surprises because, as all serious Court-watchers know, if McCleskey had been complaining that such a clear pattern of racial discrimination was interfering with his employment rights, for example, he could have pointed to a number of cases where the Court had allowed relief. But the social science evidence that would have been sufficient to save McCleskey's job was not considered sufficient to save his life. Like they say, "Death is different."

Indeed death is "different;" and in the four areas described above, that difference is presently accompanied by seemingly insurmountable barriers to the fair administration of capital punishment. If that penalty stays on the books we can all sincerely hope that those barriers may someday be conquered.

But nobody has figured out how to do it, so those good intentions won't do anything for you in your death penalty trial today. That trial is likely to be Hell; and the road to Hell is paved with good intentions.

While admitting these grievous faults should be corrected, some death penalty proponents ask why we should be unduly concerned about how we treat these vicious and depraved killers. This begs the question, for of course we don't know who the vicious and depraved killers—those who presumably deserve to die—are unless they have been accurately and fairly selected. And they forget that these faults must also be borne by those defendants who are acquitted.

PROTECTION

A friend from out west has asked me if Randy Greenawalt, on death row there, shouldn't be "eliminated" just for the safety of the rest of us . . . no other reason. A clipping he sends from the *The Denver Post* of January 20, 1997, shows that Greenawalt is a vicious and depraved killer, who being in prison for life for murder, escaped and brutally helped murder six more on a crime spree. This is a very hard case. It is also a rare one; and, paradoxically, its very rarity seems to lead people to be even more upset about it.

The facts of the case are so horrible it's hard to remember that we can't have the death penalty just for Greenawalt. The state has to draw guidelines; and experience shows that whatever guidelines are drawn for imposing death will almost surely be used by prosecutors and juries to cover a wider variety of cases than was intended, and with all the probabilities for error and unfairness described above. In fact, in the sensational cases there is more risk of error.

But, as suggested by my western friend, one could draw this very strict guideline: "People serving life for first-degree murder, if they escape and commit first-degree murder again, will be executed." Let's see how the two parts of this guideline would have applied to Greenawalt. He was in prison for life for murder, all right. According to *The Denver Post* he was in "medium security" which "offered an informal picnic setting" where his escape accomplices "had little trouble smuggling in an ice chest packed with revolvers and sawed-off shotguns." In other words, a state's incredibly lax prison administration cost six innocent persons their lives. In a properly run prison, it wouldn't have happened. To let such mistakes determine our policy on the death penalty is plainly to let the tail wag the dog.

Would that threat of execution for future killings deter someone like Greenawalt? Well it didn't deter him, did it? The evidence discussed above fails to show that the public is any safer where they have executions. Other evidence shows that some persons, usually weak minded and under stress (like many in prison), commit murder so that the State will execute them, as a means of suicide; and there are clinically documented cases of this.

Greenawalt also fits the second part of our guideline because he murdered again. Must he be executed to protect the public from him now? If he were allowed to live, you may be sure that this time the state's prison system (like other well-run penal systems) would keep him locked up tight until he dies . . . and that (as shown above) would be cheaper than executing him. There are no absolute safety guarantees in this life. But capital punishment for the Greenawalts of the world doesn't increase the odds for law-abiding citizens, it just costs them more money.

It should be emphasized that the above description of Randy Greenawalt is based solely upon my friend's newspaper clipping; and that additional facts, as developed in a recent evidentiary hearing, show him in a more sympathetic light. However, to go into these facts here would obscure the point that my friend was so vividly trying to make.

AMERICA'S ISOLATION

Every Western industrial nation except the United States has stopped executing criminals. Most of them have formally abolished the death penalty; and the few who keep it on the books never use it. America stands alone among its traditional peers in having capital punishment today. The evidence of this has only been brought together in recent years . . . since Amnesty International was awarded the Nobel Prize. The ancient nations of Europe, from whence many of our ancestors came, have repealed it. It no longer exists in Britain,

Holland, France, Scandinavia, Spain, Italy or Germany. It has been repealed in Canada and Australia and most of the countries in South America. It was abolished even in South Africa, which until recently was among the world's leading executioners. So it is not surprising that many people from abroad regard America's retention of the penalty as the indication of an innate American savagery that we refuse to address.

Some of them even come over to the United States to view our capital punishment operation, and a number of them are immensely helpful workers in our woefully understaffed criminal justice system. But one can't help but see that they tend to regard us rather like monkeys in a zoo. It doesn't seem to help much to tell them that we have problems of our own and that people everywhere tend to resort to barbarism under stress. Yes, they say, but if you grew up where every single family during the last 80 years has had some of its members brutally killed for what (from the killers' point of view) were "very good reasons," you wouldn't feel that way. We've seen you up close and there are millions of you who just love to sit in your soft chairs and hear, without any risk, about somebody being "fried." It seems almost as hard to convince them that they are wrong as it is to convince many Americans who believe in the death penalty of their mistake. But one thing is incontestably clear from the evidence: The world's main executing nations are Iraq, Iran, Nigeria, communist China and Somalia. And America seems to be among the top ten. How does it feel to be among select company like that?

Long experience teaches me that when first exposed to the evidence about the death penalty many people say, "Things can't possibly be this bad; not in America! Isn't this person misinformed or exaggerating?" I'm afraid the answer is that things are this bad . . . and sometimes worse. The evidence discussed above, and set out in the references below, show capital punishment to be nothing but hollow vengeance at high public cost.

EUGENE WANGER, a member of the Michigan bar, was a delegate to the MI Constitutional Convention of 1961–2 where he authored the state's constitutional prohibition of capital punishment. He has been co-chairman of the MI Committee Against Capital Punishment, was co-founder of the MI Coalition

Against the Death Penalty, and past national board member of the National Coalition to Abolish the Death Penalty. Mr. Wanger is a graduate of Amherst College and the University of Michigan Law School. His library on capital punishment is perhaps the largest in America in private hands.

REFERENCES

Cesare Beccaria, *On Crimes and Punishments* (1764) is available in several editions; the Paolucci (Library of Liberal Arts 1963) and Young (Hackett 1986) translations have valuable introductions.

Benjamin Rush, *Essays Literary, Moral and Philosophical* (1806); the Meranze edition (Union College 1988) contains a valuable introduction; see also

Philip English Mackey, *Voices Against Death* (Burt Franklin 1976) for expressions by Rush & his early successors.

Eugene G. Wanger, "Historical Reflections on Michigan's Abolition of the Death Penalty" (*Thomas M. Cooley Law Review* [Journal] 1997).

Raymond T. Bye, *Capital Punishment in the United States* (Yearly Meeting of Friends 1919).

Lewis E. Lawes, *Man's Judgment of Death* (Putnam's 1924), reprinted by Patterson Smith 1969; later famous for popular writings on prison reform.

E. Roy Calvert, *Capital Punishment in the Twentieth Century* (Putnam's 1927); last edition reprinted by Patterson Smith with a valuable introduction 1973; perhaps most eloquent.

Thorsten Sellin, *The Death Penalty* (American Law Institute 1959); see also his *Capital Punishment* (Harper & Row 1967) & *The Penalty of Death* (Sage 1980); until his death perhaps America's greatest criminologist.

Hugo Adam Bedau, *The Death Penalty in America* (the Anchor 1964, Aldine 1967 & Oxford 1982 editions differ substantially); a 4th Edition of this superb reference will soon be issued by Oxford.

William J. Bowers. *Legal Homicide* (Northeastern 1984); studies of deterrence, brutalization, discrimination; lists American state executions.

Stephen Nathanson, *An Eye for an Eye* (Rowman & Littlefield 1987); strong philosophical & deterrence analysis.

Kenneth C. Hass & James A. Inciardi, *Challenging Capital Punishment* (Sage 1988); studies of deterrence, error, brutalization, fairness.

William Bailey & Ruth Peterson, "Murder and Capital Punishment in the Evolving Context of the Post-Furman Era" (*Social Forces* [Journal] 1988); reviews deterrence studies.

Roger Hood, *The Death Penalty* (2nd Edition Oxford 1996); world view, deterrence.

Welsh S. White, *The Death Penalty in the Nineties* (Michigan 1991); fairness, discrimination.

Charles L. Black, Jr., *Capital Punishment: The Inevitability of Caprice and Mistake* (2nd Edition Norton 1981); seminal legal analysis.

Hugo Adam Bedau & Michael L. Radelet, "Miscarriages of Justice in Potentially Capital Cases" (*Stanford Law Review* [Journal] 1987).

Michael L. Radelet, Hugo Adam Bedau & Constance E. Putnam, *In Spite of Innocence* (Northeastern 1992).

U.S. House Judiciary Subcommittee Staff Report, *Innocence and the Death Penalty: Assessing the Danger of Mistaken Executions* (Death Penalty Information Center 1993); adds even more cases.

NAACP Legal Defense and Educational Fund, Inc., *Death Row, U.S.A.* ([Journal] Summer 1996); a quarterly long the best source of American death row statistics.

Darrell K. Gilliard, et al, *Prison and Jail Inmates* (U.S. Bureau of Justice Statistics Bulletin 1995); a standard source of American prisoner statistics, updated periodically.

Philip J. Cook & Donna B. Slawson, *The Costs of Processing Murder Cases in North Carolina* (Duke University 1993); the most complete & professional of many cost studies showing that capital punishment is more expensive than life imprisonment.

Richard C. Dieter, *Millions Misspent: What Politicians Don't Say about the High Costs of the Death Penalty* (Death Penalty Information Center 1992); valuable reference.

Ronald J. Tabak, et al, "Is There Any Habeas Left in This Corpus" (*Loyola University Chicago Law Journal* [Journal] 1996); valuable on fairness, error.

Richard C. Dieter, *With Justice for Few: The Growing Crisis in Death Penalty Representation* (Death Penalty Information Center 1995); valuable reference.

David C. Baldus, et al, *Equal Justice and the Death Penalty* (Northeastern 1990).

Amnesty International, *When the State Kills . . .* (Amnesty International USA 1989); world view.

Amnesty International, *Amnesty International Report 1995* (Amnesty International USA 1995) updates world view.

The foregoing is reprinted from Mr. Wanger's chapter in *Frontiers of Justice, Volume 1: The Death Penalty* (Brunswick, Maine: Biddle Publishing Co., 1997).

21. Will Innocent Persons Be Executed?—Another Perspective

Michael Radelet

Scholarly research on the administration of capital punishment in the United States has reached a nearly unanimous conclusion: Those who enforce the death penalty are making godlike decisions without godlike skills.

There have now been at least 75 men and women since 1970 who have been released from America's death rows because of probable innocence.

Earlier this month, 30 of these former inmates gathered at Northwestern Law School in Chicago. One by one they walked onto the stage and introduced themselves to the 1,000 conference attendees.

"Hello, my name is Joseph Green Brown. In 1974 I was sentenced to death for a murder that I did not commit. If the State of Florida had gotten its way, I would be dead today."

In retrospect, Brown and his 74 colleagues were incredibly lucky. In his case, the sole witness against him eventually came forward and admitted perjury. The Eleventh Circuit Court of Appeals later ordered a new trial because of this and prosecutorial suppression of exculpatory evidence.

After nearly 14 years on death row, and once coming to within 13 hours of execution, Brown was released.

And luck it is. Anyone who cynically argues that these cases show "the system works" by being able to detect its mistakes knows nothing about how these exonerations occur. If the system "worked," most of these 75 people would be dead.

Then, among other things, there would then be no venue in which their innocence could be established.

The 75 men and women on this sad list come from throughout the country. Most are minorities and poor, and were easy targets for the state to convict. Undoubtedly, if these 75 men and women were the children of judges or legislators, instead of children of the poor, the death penalty would be relegated to history books.

Kirk Bloodsworth from Maryland was there. The victim in his case was not only murdered but also raped; so, luckily for Bloodsworth, the real killer left crucial evidence. DNA analysis of the rape evidence in 1993 eventually proved Bloodsworth's innocence.

Rolando Cruz from Illinois was there; he was saved in part by a conscientious prosecutor who quit her job rather than pursuing what she recognized as a travesty.

Walter McMillian was there; he was released from Alabama's death row only when "60 Minutes" came to town, reinvestigated the facts and definitively proved his innocence.

And errors even happen close to home. In 1983, Willie Brown and Larry Troy were sentenced to death for killing a fellow prisoner in Raiford. A few years later, Mr. Brown's girlfriend, with considerable help from the FDLE and Gainesville attorney Bill Salmon, met the chief accuser at the Greyhound Bus Station here in Gainesville.

The witness, not realizing the girlfriend was wearing a legally-authorized wire, admitted perjuring himself. In 1988, the Gainesville state attorney's office dropped the murder charges against the two men.

Several former death row inmates with strong evidence of innocence were not there. They have been executed.

Pedro Medina, a member of Westminster Presbyterian Church here in Gainesville, is one of them. Despite appeals for clemency from the daughter of the murder victim, who never thought Medina was guilty, Medina was literally burned to death in Florida's electric chair in 1997.

And Jesse Tafero was not there. He, too, met a fiery death in Florida's electric chair. But his codefendant, Sonia Jacobs, was in Chicago. She was convicted on the same evidence that sent Tafero to the hereafter. After his death she was able to find abundant evidence of both her and Jesse's innocence in the files of the prosecutor who sent them to death row.

In the next couple of weeks, the United States will execute its 500th prisoner since Gary Gilmore and John Spenkelink were killed in the late 1970s. With 75 documented cases of innocence, that means that we find one innocent person for each six or seven we execute. If we found rodent parts in each sixth hot dog we ate, few of us would still eat hot dogs.

Perhaps someday we will learn what virtually every other industrialized country in the world has already learned: The question is no longer "Who deserves to die?" The real question is "Who deserves to kill?"

Michael L. Radelet is professor and chair of the Department of Sociology at the University of Florida.

The Gainesville Sun OPINIONS, Sunday, November 29, 1998.

22. Michigan's Historic Ban of Capital Punishment

Michigan, by statute in 1846, was the first government in the English-speaking world to abolish capital punishment for murder and lesser crimes. The effort was led by Austin Blair (later to be Michigan's great Republican Civil War Governor) and others.

This was the first success in the campaign begun years earlier by the American Patriot, Signer of the Declaration of Independence and staunch Christian, Dr. Benjamin Rush of Philadelphia to abolish the death penalty in the United States.

Our state has never restored it. Article IV, Section 46, of Michigan's 1963 Constitution says "No law shall be enacted providing for the penalty of death." This provision was added by the state's 1961–62 Constitutional Convention. Two-thirds of the 144 delegates to that Convention were Republican, most of them very conservative; yet this provision passed that Convention with only three dissenting votes.

The recommendation of the Constitutional Convention's Legislative Powers Committee in part stated:

"The compelling arguments against capital punishment were succinctly re-stated in the *Journal of the American Judicature Society* for October, 1958, as follows:

1. The evidence clearly shows that execution does not act as a deterrent to capital crimes.
2. The serious offenses are committed, except in rare instances, by those suffering from mental disturbances; are impulsive in nature; and are not the acts of the 'criminal' class.
3. Conviction of the innocent does occur and death makes a miscarriage of justice irrevocable.
4. When the death sentence is removed as a possible punishment, more convictions are possible with less delays.
5. Unequal application of the law takes place because those executed are often the poor, the ignorant, and the unfortunate without resources.
6. The state sets a bad example when it takes a life. Imitative crimes and murder are stimulated by executions.
7. Legally taking a life is useless and demoralizing to the general public. It is also demoralizing to the public officials who, dedicated to rehabilitating individuals, must callously put a man to death. The effect upon fellow prisoners can be imagined.
8. A trial where a life may be at stake is highly sensationalized, adversely affects the administration of justice, and is bad for the community.
9. Society is amply protected by a sentence of life imprisonment.

"The Committee believes that it is both fitting and opportune for Michigan to step forward in the tradition which we began over 115 years ago and that the adoption of this provision would be a significant contribution to the concept of civilized justice which all of us seek to serve."

Since that Convention 37 years ago, many additional facts have come to light which strongly support the Convention's arguments.

Throughout the years, Michigan's penalty for first-degree murder has been—and is—<u>mandatory</u> life in prison without the right to parole. Only if the Governor uses his Constitutional powers of mercy to commute the sentence is a convicted first-degree murderer in Michigan even eligible for parole consideration.

Today, apart from Michigan and 12 sister abolition states (including the District of Columbia), America is the only Western industrialized nation to retain the death penalty. A majority of all the nations of the world have now abolished capital punishment—either de jure or de facto—and Michigan has led the way. It would internationally be regarded as a tragedy if our state restored it.

A century ago Michigan's great jurist and legal scholar Thomas M. Cooley, when questioned about capital punishment, said:

> The fundamental objection to the taking of human life by law is found in the tendency to destroy in men's minds the sense of the sacredness of life. . . . Mankind are not to be impressed with the priceless value of existence by spectacles of deliberate executions, and so long as the state justifies the taking of life for crime against society, individuals will frame in their own minds excuses for taking it for offenses real or imaginary against themselves.

The above history is documented in *Cooley Law Review* 13/3 (1996): 755–774. The international data is summarized in *Georgia St. Univ. Law Review* 14/2 (1998): 429–430. The Constitutional Convention's report and debates appear on pages 595–598 and 2968 of its two-volume *Official Record*.

Courtesy of Michigan Committee Against Capital Punishment.

23. The Co$t of Capital Puni$hment

Many Michigan people are surprised to learn that the death penalty costs more than life imprisonment. How can that be, they wonder, thinking of the inmates that won't have to be fed and housed.

In fact, if Michigan revives the death penalty, it will cost state and county taxpayers far more than they can save. Millions more annually, because the added costs of the death penalty are staggering.

SMALL SAVINGS

The only money you can be sure to save by executing an inmate is the marginal cost of his or her imprisonment—about the cost of that inmate's food, clothing & laundry. At 1998 prices that marginal cost—or "variable cost" as it's called—is less than $2,500 a year. (Estimate by Wm. Kime, Retired Deputy Director, Mich. Dept. of. Corrections, *Life and Death Economic Issues*, 1990, adjusted for inflation.)

By executing someone you cannot save the "average cost" of their imprisonment, determined by dividing total prison operating costs by the total number of inmates, because those executed are too few to reduce fixed costs like staffing, programs, utilities and maintenance. Suppose you executed six people a year? The Michigan prison population—now about 43,000—goes up or down by more than that almost every day.

For the same reason it's doubtful that executions could save on prison construction costs. The above savings (even if you figure them at their "average cost") are far exceeded by the increased *prison* and *litigation* costs of the death penalty.

INCREASED PRISON COSTS

Richard McGee, administrator of California corrections, years ago wrote, "The actual costs of execution, the cost of operating the super-maximum security condemned unit, the years spent by some inmates in condemned status, and a pro-rata share of top level prison officials' time spent in administering the unit add up to a cost substantially greater than the cost to retain them in prison for the rest of their lives." 28 *Federal Probation* 13–14 (1964) In addition, Michigan would have to build a condemned unit and execution facilities.

"Furthermore," McGee added, "perhaps half of those condemned could make highly useful prisoners . . . [They] would more than pay for both their own keep and that of the other half."

INCREASED LITIGATION COSTS

The added litigation costs of the death penalty are immense. Two trials are required instead of one (the first to determine guilt, the second to set the penalty). All 8 stages of the process (investigation, indictment, pre-trial, trial, sentencing, appeal, post-conviction and clemency) take far longer and cost much more. The sensational publicity invites it and the life at stake demands it.

Almost always the taxpayer must pay the defense cost, as well as the prosecution cost, because the defendant is indigent. Contrary to many homicide cases, no defendant pleads guilty in a death penalty case except the suicidal. In Michigan a death penalty defense system would also have to be created.

A 1993 Duke University study, *The Costs of Processing Murder Cases in North Carolina*, estimated that these net extra death penalty expenses were costing that state over $2 million per execution. Earlier studies calculated these extra costs totaled $90 million per year in California and would total $118 million in New Nork annually. Texas taxpayers were paying an average of $2.3 million per death penalty case, which was about three times the cost of life imprisonment for 40 years there. In Florida each execution was costing the state an extra $3.2 million; and at the end of 1988 it had spent $57.2 million to execute 18 people. Dieter, *Millions Misspent: What Politicians Don't Say about the High Costs of the Death Penalty* (1992).

Meanwhile, the American Bar Association reported that "the justice system in many parts of the United States is on the verge of collapse due to inadequate funding . . ." *Funding the Justice System: A Call to Action* (1992).

Would it be worth these extra millions for Michigan to execute these killers instead of sentencing them to life in prison without parole, especially since we are certain to make a mistake now and then?

Courtesy of Michigan Committee Against Capital Punishment.

24. Documentation for MCACP "The Co$t of Capital Puni$hment" Issue Paper

1. Wm. Kime, Retired Dep. Dir. MiDept. Corrections, *Life and Death Economic Issues* memo of 4/16/90.
2. Inflation adjustment sheet for same from web.
3. McGee, CAP PUN AS SEEN BY A CORRECTIONAL ADMINISTRATOR, 28 Fed. Probation #2 (June 1964) pp. 11–16.
4. USGAO, LIMITED DATA AVAILABLE ON COSTS OF DEATH PENALTY, GAO/GGD-89-122, Sept. 1989, pp. 3–4.
5. Cook & Slawson, COSTS OF PROCESSING MURDER CASES IN NC, Duke U. Study, 1993, pp. 98–99.
6. Dieter (DPIC), MILLIONS MISSPENT: WHAT POLITICIANS DON'T SAY ABOUT THE HIGH COST OF THE DEATH PEN, (1992) PP. i, 3–4, 7–8, 14. You should get this study.
7. Sobelsohn, DEATH PENALTY: DOLLARS AND SENSE, Detroit Free Press op ed article 7/31/86.

25. Testimony of Eugene G. Wanger

MICHIGAN SENATE JUDICIARY COMMITTEE HEARING ON
THE DEATH PENALTY, PONTIAC, MARCH 23, 1999

*This testimony was also presented at a Legislative Committee Hearing,
Lansing, April 19–20, 1999.*

My name is Eugene G. Wanger. Since 1972 I have been co-chairman, with Tom Downs, of the Michigan Committee Against Capital Punishment.

We urge you to oppose the proposed Joint Resolutions which, if adopted, would produce an election to bring the death penalty back to Michigan. Because the resulting campaign would waste an immense amount of time, attention, effort and money which could otherwise be used to develop effective ways to fight and prevent crime, because the public is so poorly informed about the issue, and because the death penalty is so harmful and repulsive, we believe that putting it on the ballot would be a very wrong thing to do.

Michigan by statute in 1846—following the lead of the American Patriot and Signer of the Declaration of Independence, Dr. Benjamin Rush of

Philadelphia—was the first government in the English-speaking world to abolish the death penalty for murder and lesser crimes, and we have never restored it. Since 1963, Michigan's constitution has prohibited it.

Thirty-eight years ago, I authored that prohibition when I was privileged to be one of the 144 delegates elected to Michigan's Constitutional Convention. Two-thirds of those 144 delegates were Republican, most of them very conservative; yet that proposal to outlaw the death penalty passed the Convention with only 3 dissenting votes. The Convention's Committee Report called it "a significant contribution to the concept of civilized justice."

Today according to United Nations' figures, a majority of all the nations on earth have followed Michigan's lead and abandoned the death penalty, either de jure or de facto. For example, Britain, France, Germany, Italy, Belgium, Holland, Scandinavia, Portugal, Spain, South Africa, Russia, Australia, Canada and Mexico have all abolished it. America (except for Michigan and her 12 sister abolition states, including the District of Columbia) stands side by side with Iraq, Iran, Communist China, Nigeria and Somalia as one of the principal executing nations of the world.

Today also, Michigan hears cries for the revival of the death penalty, a penalty which even for the most heinous crimes lowers society to the level of the criminal and feeds the lust for blood revenge which is present, to a greater or lesser degree, in all of us. It is a very rare murder which equals the psychological torture and pain of an execution. Except for the fact that they have been legalized, executions are the most cold-blooded, premeditated murders in the world. Their brutalizing effect upon society is evident; and as Michigan's great jurist Thomas M. Cooley said a century ago,

". . . so long as the state justifies the taking of life for crime against society, individuals will frame in their own minds excuses for taking if for offenses real or imaginary against themselves . . ."

Most of you are aware that the death penalty does not deter murder better than life imprisonment does; and that regardless of whether you are a policeman, prison guard or ordinary citizen, you are no safer from being a victim of homicide where they have the death penalty. Moreover, in prison and out, the death penalty acts on some unbalanced minds as an incitement to kill—and there are documented cases of this. These killers may be insane, but their victims are just as dead.

No one who has followed the national news for the past few months—especially as reported by *The New York Times* and *The Chicago Tribune*—can be ignorant of the now overwhelming evidence that in death penalty states they occasionally execute the innocent. The main causes are mistaken eyewitness identification, perjured testimony, false confessions and sometimes official misconduct. I understand some Michigan death penalty advocates to say that these unfortunate dead are merely "casualties of War." We submit that even in War, it is only the cruel or ignorant commander who sacrifices his troops needlessly.

As you know, Michigan's penalty for first-degree murder has been—and is—mandatory life in prison without the right to parole. Only if the Governor uses his Constitutional powers of mercy to commute the sentence is a convicted first-degree murderer in Michigan even eligible for parole consideration. That is a very severe penalty. While it may not be severe enough to satisfy some, we submit that the added margin of satisfaction they might derive from the death penalty is something we cannot afford.

If Michigan revives the death penalty, it will cost state and county taxpayers far more than they can save. Millions more annually. About all you can save by executing an inmate is the cost of his or her food, clothing and laundry, which is less than $2,500 a year. This is because those executed are too few in number to reduce fixed prison costs like staffing, programs, utilities and maintenance.

On the other hand, the additional prison and litigation costs of the death penalty are immense, as shown by studies in death penalty states.

A 1993 Duke University study estimated that these net extra death penalty expenses were costing North Carolina over $2 million per execution. Earlier studies calculated that these extra costs totaled $90 million per year in California and would total $118 million in New York annually. Texas taxpayers were paying an average of $2.3 million per death penalty case, which was about three times the cost of life imprisonment there. In Florida each execution was costing the state an extra $3.2 million; and at the end of 1988 it had spent

$57.2 million to execute 18 people. In addition, Michigan would have to build a death row, execution facilities and a legal support system for them from scratch. In light of society's other needs and our limited resources, this is too great a price to pay.

It is a commonplace of history that civilization tends to resort to barbarism under stress. We ask you to help prevent that from happening in Michigan by voting against these proposed Joint Resolutions. Thank you for your kind attention.

26. Would the Death Penalty for "Cop Killers" Help the Police?

Some people who want to revive the death penalty in Michigan—a state which has been without that penalty for 153 years—have suggested that we should at least have it for those who murder police officers. It should therefore be pointed out that a good deal of research has been done on this subject. This research reveals the following three things:

1. The evidence fails to show that a police officer is any safer from being a victim of homicide where they have the death penalty.
2. The odds of convicting and executing an innocent person are much greater in "cop killer" cases.
3. In some situations, the death penalty makes a police officer's life more dangerous.

As Professors William Bailey and Ruth Peterson pointed out in 1987, if capital punishment deterred, "one would expect yearly police-killing rates to be significantly higher in abolitionist than in death penalty states and significantly lower in retentionist jurisdictions making greater use of the death sentence for murder." Yet they concluded that "Not for a single year was evidence found that police are safer in jurisdictions that provide for capital punishment. Nor did the analysis produce a single instance where higher levels of death sentences are associated significantly with lower rates of police killings." (CRIMINOLOGY, Vol. 25, No. 1, pp. 8, 22)

In 1998 these same researchers concluded that "if the killing of a police officer means a higher risk of receiving a death sentence and being executed, as is the case in the U. S. in recent years (compared to citizen killings), then the death penalty should be noticeably effective in deterring police killings. But here too the evidence is negative. Capital punishment does not appear to provide police officers with an added measure of protection against being murdered." (Acker, et al [Editors], AMERICA'S EXPERIMENT WITH CAPITAL PUNISHMENT, Carolina Academic Press, p. 173)

Moreover, as reported by Professor Samuel Gross of the University of Michigan Law School on May 5, 1999, in a memorandum prepared for this report, "although cop killers constitute fewer than 4% of the death row population in this country, they make up about 9% of those who were released from death row because of innocence" and that "*defendants who are sentenced to death for killing police officers are more than two-and-a-half times more likely to be innocent than defendants who are sentenced to death for other murders.*" From 1972 to the end of 1998, at least 75 prisoners have been released from death row in America "because their innocence was proven, or (in a few cases) because of severe factual doubts about their guilt," he noted. (Emphasis supplied)

The reason for this greater margin of error appears to lie in the nature of police killer cases: "Murders of police officers have all the characteristics of the subset of murder cases that are most likely to produce miscarriages of justice," continues Professor Gross. "They are highly visible; they are very disturbing; they are likely to result in intense political and institutional pressure to solve the crime and bring the killer to justice." (ERRONEOUS CONVICTIONS IN CAPITAL PROSECUTIONS FOR KILLING POLICE OFFICERS, available from the Michigan Committee Against Capital Punishment)

Finally, it has long been known that the death penalty sometimes incites additional killings by mentally unstable persons, who seek suicide by execution and commit murder so that the state will execute them, and by terrorist fanatics seeking martyrdom. For these people—such as the psychopath who is tired of living and wants to go out 'in a blaze of glory'—capital punishment for those who kill police makes every police officer a target. (Sellin, THE DEATH PENALTY, American Law Institute, 1959, pp. 65–69; articles by Drs. West, Solomon & Diamond in the AMERICAN JOURNAL OF ORTHO-PSYCHIATRY, Vol. 45, No. 4, 1975; pp. 689–722; Dr. Hacker, CRUSADERS, CRIMINALS, CRAZIES, W. W. Norton & Co., 1976, pp. 95, 316, 338).

Courtesy of Michigan Committee Against Capital Punishment.

27. Documentation for "Would the Death Penalty for 'Cop Killers' Help the Police?"

1. William C. Bailey & Ruth D. Peterson, POLICE KILLINGS AND CAPITAL PUNISHMENT: THE POST-FURMAN PERIOD, 25 Criminology 1–25, at 8, 22 (Issue No. 1, 1987)
2. Ruth D. Peterson & William C. Bailey, IS CAPITAL PUNISHMENT AN EFFECTIVE DETERRENT FOR MURDER? AN EXAMINATON OF SOCIAL SCIENCE RESEARCH, being Chapter 6 of Acker, Bohm & Lanier (Eds.), AMERICA'S EXPERIMENT WITH CAPITAL PUNISHMENT, Carolina Academic Press, 1998, 157–182, at 172–173
3. Samuel R. Gross, ERRONEOUS CONVICTIONS IN CAPITAL PROSECUTIONS FOR KILLING POLICE OFFICERS, May 5, 1999, University of Michigan Law School, 2 pp.
4. Thorsten Sellin, THE DEATH PENALTY, The American Law Institute, 1959, pp. 65–69.
5. Louis Joylon West, M.D., PSYCHIATRIC REFLECTIONS ON THE DEATH PENALTY, George F. Solomon, M.D., CAPITAL PUNISHMENT AS SUICIDE AND AS MURDER, Bernard L. Diamond, MURDER AND THE DEATH PENALTY: A CASE

REPORT, all published in 45 *American Journal of Orthopsychiatry* 689–722 (Issue No. 4, July 1975) and reprinted in Bedau & Pierce (Eds.), CAPITAL PUNISHMENT IN THE UNITED STATES, AMS Press, Inc., 1976, at pp. 419–457.

6. Frederick J. Hacker, M.D., CRUSADERS, CRIMINALS, CRAZIES, W. W. Norton & Company, Inc., 1976, pp. 95, 316, 338.

28. Michiganians Speak Out on the Death Penalty

Published on page one of the *New York Times* on September 22, 2000, an article by Raymond Bonner and Ford Fessenden quoted many Americans who lived in states that did not have the death penalty, explaining why they were against the practice.

Of special interest to people in Michigan were the statements of its conservative Republican governor, John Engler, who was known to oppose capital punishment but had never said very much about it. Basing his opinion on both moral and pragmatic grounds, he said that the state had made "a wise decision" in repealing the death penalty 150 years previously, and added, "We're pretty proud of the fact that we don't have the death penalty."

Engler was not influenced by opinion polls that showed 60% of Michiganians were for capital punishment, saying that 100% of them would like not to pay taxes.

Also emphasized was the state's constitutional provision outlawing the penalty, which had been authored by Eugene G. Wanger at Michigan's constitutional convention in 1961. Wanger pointed out that the convention was heavily Republican, most very conservative, and that the death penalty ban passed with only three dissenting votes.

John O'Hair, highly respected long-time prosecutor from Detroit, was quoted at length about the bad example a state sets by taking life and that it is not a deterrent of any consequence to murders. If some citizens want vengeance, O'Hair said, 'life in prison without parole is about as punitive as you can get." The state's mandatory penalty for first-degree murder is life without the possibility of parole.

Matthew Davis of the Michigan Department of Corrections emphasized that the state's 2,572 inmates serving life without parole cause fewer problems than the general prison population. They are quieter, less insolent, and more likely to obey the rules, he said. Bringing the death penalty back "may not be the most effective use of the people's money," Mr. Davis added, because "that pound of flesh comes at a higher price than a lifetime of incarceration."

[The use here of this abstract instead of including the original article, is explained in the preface.]

Raymond Bonner and Ford Fessenden, "Absence of Executions:
A Special Report . . . ," *New York Times*, September 22, 2000.

29. How States Stack Up on Death: Death Penalty and Homicide Rates

Published in the *New York Times* on September 22, 2000, under the title, "Deadly Statistics: A Survey of Crime and Punishment," this brief article by Ford Fessenden emphasized that homicide rates in the states with the death penalty are higher than in those without.

Examining the 12 abolition states and the 36 death penalty states, the paper's analysis found that the homicide rates did not decline any more in the states that instituted the death penalty.

Indeed, the homicide rates in the two groups of states have shown similar up-and-down trends over the years, the *New York Times* survey found . . . evidence that something other than capital punishment laws drives homicides. Actually, rates went down more in the states that had not had executions.

The Times used the type of analysis that criminologists have been using since the 1930s. It quoted the econometrician Prof. Isaac Ehrlich as saying that that approach was "devoid of scientific merit." However, "most criminologists," said the *Times*, "discount Professor Ehrlich's work."

[The use here of this abstract instead of including the original article, is explained in the preface.]

Ford Fessenden, "Deadly Statistics: A Survey of Crime and Punishment," *New York Times*, September 22, 2000.

30. Michigan & Capital Punishment

Eugene G. Wanger

Several years ago a legislator in Texas was asked if he would vote to abolish capital punishment. "No," he replied, "capital punishment was good enough for my father and it's good enough for me."

That could not have happened in Michigan, for our state, by statute in 1846, was the first government in the English-speaking world to abolish capital punishment for murder and lesser crimes. Our state has never restored it. Since 1964, Michigan's constitution has prohibited it.

Today, following Michigan's lead, a majority of all the nations on earth— including Canada, Mexico, England, Scandinavia, and almost all of Europe— have abolished the death penalty, either de jure or de facto; but America (with the exception of Michigan and 12 other states) is one of the world's principal executing nations. Since 1998, only Communist China and the Congo have executed more people than the United States. Iraq and Iran are not far behind.

What has created this unique and paradoxical situation? How did Michigan come to abolish the death penalty so early, and how has that position been maintained?

The initial inspiration seems to have come from the eighteenth-century

European Enlightenment. That was a time when the criminal law of civilized countries everywhere was ferocious, imposing torture and death for dozens— and in England as many as 200—of even the most trivial crimes.

Human life was cheap, especially if it was the life of the lowly. Executions were common entertainment. Men and sometimes women were executed without qualms and with dispatch, normally after rapid and perfunctory proceedings. As Alexander Pope said,

The hungry Judges soon the Sentence sign,
And Wretches hang that Jury-men may Dine.

Does all of this seem to you like a very long time ago? Then talk to Bette Hulbert, recently retired director of the Michigan Historical Museum, who remembers her great-grandmother telling her of being taken when she was a little schoolgirl in Northern France to the center of town with the other children to see a man have his limbs each tied to one of four "big white horses" that then "just kept going" until they pulled him apart.

Put the scaffold on the Commons,
Where the multitude can meet;
All the schools and ladies summon,
Let them all enjoy the treat.

In London, where picking pockets was a hanging offense, pickpockets plied their trade with greatest success at the public hangings, when everyone else was "looking up"; and as late as 1807, at a triple hanging outside the Old Bailey, the pressure of the crowd to see the final struggles of the condemned was so great that 30 of the spectators were crushed to death at the foot of the gallows. A publication of the time even gives their names and addresses.

In combating these and other evils for almost a hundred years, the philosophes, as the leaders of the Enlightenment were called, assiduously promoted a highly critical attitude toward the authority of the past and inculcated a powerfully optimistic view that the lot of humanity could be vastly improved through the application of human reason.

When the ideas of the Enlightenment swept across the Atlantic Ocean, they became well known to the leaders of the American Colonies. Here, unlike in England, there were only about a dozen crimes punishable by death. And here in the Colonies it troubled many to think, or be told, that among other things the death penalty might violate fundamental principles of Christianity.

The death penalty abolition campaign was begun by the American patriot, staunch Christian, signer of the Declaration of Independence, and eminent physician, Benjamin Rush of Philadelphia. He was the first American to speak out against the penalty of death for murder, which he did in a paper he read at Benjamin Franklin's house on March 9, 1787, and in an essay published in *The American Museum* magazine for July of the following year.

Rush widely distributed these essays and the campaign to abolish the death penalty in America was on. Many brilliant and talented reform leaders joined the fray, concentrating mainly in New England, New York, and Pennsylvania. The first success, however, was achieved in the wilds of Michigan. Peopled largely by immigrants from New York and New England, and with little experience of executions, Michigan Territory held a disagreeably traumatic hanging in Detroit in 1830. The following January, Governor Lewis Cass—still considered Michigan's greatest public servant—told the Territory's Legislative Council, "The period is probably not far distant, when it will be universally acknowledged, that all the just objects of human laws may be fully answered, without the infliction of capital punishment."

Four years later, Michigan initially grappled with the capital punishment question when writing its first state Constitution in 1835. On the fourth day of the Constitutional Convention, one committee proposed a constitution stating in part, "Capital punishment ought not to be inflicted; the true design of all punishment being to reform; not to exterminate mankind."

But the proposal was not adopted, and a prevailing sentiment in the brief debate appeared to be that the state was as yet unprepared to "make all necessary and adequate provision for the safe and sure confinement of criminals." Michigan's capital punishment abolitionists, however, would soon be back.

The next few years saw them conduct several legislative skirmishes without result, and in about 1840, Michiganians learned that the Canadians had hanged an innocent man three years before just across the river in what is now Windsor, the true culprit later having made a death-bed confession of his guilt.

In 1844, a joint committee of the Michigan Senate and House issued a report urging that the death penalty be abolished, but the committee's minority disagreed and the House sided with them by a vote of 34 to 10. In the report a substantial space is devoted to whether government has the theoretical right to impose the death penalty, a question involving the fundamental nature of government itself. Such basic questions were much on the minds of our American forebears as they settled this new land.

It is interesting that both sides went out of their way to support the religious argument (the majority taking over a page to do so), while at the same time saying that it was not really relevant to the debate. This argument, which was a dominant theme in the capital punishment abolition movement, generally pitted the hopeful injunctions of the four Christian Gospels against the ancient and somber poetry of Genesis 9:6, which advises, "Whoso sheddeth man's blood, by man shall his blood be shed."

The abolitionist majority barely mentioned the deterrence argument at all, although they could have cited a number of authorities from the Eastern States. On the other hand, the committee minority, who favored the death penalty, expressly rested their entire case on the deterrence argument.

In 1846, victory in Michigan was at hand as the legislature undertook a general revision of all the state's laws, including its lengthy criminal code. The state's determined capital punishment abolitionists were ready. They were apparently led by Democratic Senator Charles P. Bush, later a prominent Lansingite, and by Whig House-member Austin Blair, who later became Michigan's great Republican Civil War governor. Blair, who chaired the House Judiciary Committee, would later recall that his contribution to the death penalty's demise was "among the best pieces of work" that he ever did.

Equally dedicated were Senator Flavius Littlejohn, who was later a Whig candidate for governor, judge, and noted Michigan historical author and Senator William T. Howell, then president pro tem of the Senate, who was later appointed by President Lincoln to be Associate Justice of the Arizona Territory and who authored its first code of laws.

Even with such leadership, getting rid of "death" for first-degree murder was more easily said than done, but after much skirmishing, that penalty was finally fixed at "solitary confinement at hard labor in the state prison for life." As long-time political observer and retired Wayne County judge James Lincoln said, it looked like the Senate held the whole criminal code hostage until the House came around. One enthusiastic supporter from the Eastern States reported, "The sun has risen in the West!"

Shortly afterwards, a condemned murderer awaiting execution at Michigan's new prison in Jackson was pardoned when the death-bed confession of the real killer showed he was innocent and the new law providing for life imprisonment for murder instead of death became effective on March 1, 1847.

How did this remarkable, unprecedented change happen? In the absence of better evidence, we seem to be forced back upon the eighteenth-century proposition that these abolitionists, following the tradition of the Enlightenment, were rational people who simply took the arguments and evidence for capital punishment, weighed them in the balance of human reason, and found them wanting. If this is so, the implications are profound.

Four years after capital punishment was abolished, Michigan held its second constitutional convention. The "Con-Con" of 1850 was the first Michigan public body to have its debates reported verbatim and several of them were lively. A committee proposed that the death penalty be prohibited, but the proposal was rejected.

The arguments most often voiced were that the subject should be left to the legislature and that including it in the constitution would cause the people to reject the document. One delegate noted that historically even Catherine the Great, of Russia, had to restore the death penalty, citing as his authority "Boccacio, on crimes." Another delegate, with unblushing candor, said that he was mightily sorry the whole subject had come up, but that since it had he was going to vote for it anyway.

Between 1846 and the end of the century, several efforts to restore capital punishment in Michigan met with no success and the state's officials were frequently asked for their views. Austin Blair was quoted at length by the great John Bright in the British House of Commons in 1864, and letters from several Michigan prison officials were published confirming that Michigan's abolition had not raised the murder rate.

In 1881, an elderly black woman, perhaps Michigan's all-time greatest fighter for human rights, the famed Sojourner Truth, told our legislature, which was then about to vote on whether to bring the death penalty back, "We are the makers of murderers if we do it." And in 1891, Michigan's greatest judge and legal scholar, the internationally renowned Thomas M. Cooley, wrote:

> The fundamental objection to the taking of human life by law is found in the tendency to destroy in men's minds the sense of the sacredness of life and to accustom them to regard without fear or horror its destruction. . . . Mankind are not to be impressed with the priceless value of existence by spectacles of deliberate executions, and so long as the state justifies the taking of life for crime against society, individuals will frame in their own minds excuses for taking it for offenses real or imaginary against themselves, or will take it without excuse when it stands in the way of their desires.

Sojourner Truth had said it all in 10 words the decade before.

The death penalty wasn't even mentioned at our state's constitutional convention of 1908. But as the flapper era dawned and prohibition put bootlegging on a business-like basis, crime rates began to rise. An irate Michigan legislature passed a death penalty bill with a referendum provision in 1931, which was soundly rejected by a vote of the people. Frank Murphy and Henry Ford were among the notable Michiganians against it.

By 1956, the Michigan House or Senate had voted eight times for capital punishment during the twentieth century. As the sixth decade of the century approached, voices began to be heard that Michigan's much-amended 1908 state constitution should be revised, and 144 delegates were elected by the people to a constitutional convention for that purpose in 1961.

Although the state's electorate was equally divided between the two major parties, two-thirds of the delegates it elected were Republican, most very conservative. So far as is known, neither the candidates nor anyone else had suggested that capital punishment was a subject for constitutional treatment. Certainly it had never entered the mind of the convention's youngest Republican delegate, who was elected from the city of Lansing.

Ignorant of almost all the foregoing history, this delegate, only three years a lawyer, inspired by a law journal article on the death penalty that he picked up at law school and now found in his file, drafted a proposal—the only one on the subject as it turned out—which by an unusual turn came before the committee he was on. He drafted the final language, wrote the committee report, and even organized the floor debate supporting it. It passed the convention with only three dissenting votes. This would not have happened without the steadfast support of convention vice-president and leader of the Democratic delegates, Tom Downs, and the language, "No law shall be enacted providing for the penalty of death," became part of the Michigan constitution.

Eight years later, the United States Supreme Court decided *Furman v Georgia*, finding the death penalty as then administered in America to be unconstitutional. In another four years, the Supreme Court decided *Gregg*, legalizing that penalty under different procedures. During all these years, the crime rates had been rising and the public suddenly seemed more frustrated, fearful, and angry than it had been in a long time.

Calls for restoring the death penalty in Michigan were heard and after the proponents of execution failed in the legislature, the first of four statewide petition drives was started to repeal the constitutional ban. The State Board of Canvassers and the courts, however, aided by the volunteer legal services of election law expert Tom Downs, determined that the petitions lacked sufficient signatures. About three years ago, another try was made in the legislature that resoundingly failed, and Michigan's historic ban of capital punishment remains.

Over the decades, more than a dozen principal arguments have been made against the death penalty in America; but for the past few years, most of the attention seems to be concentrating upon these three:

1. It now appears to be a moral certainty, especially in the light of recent DNA evidence, that we are occasionally executing the innocent.
2. Around the world, and especially in Europe, capital punishment is increasingly viewed as a violation of basic international human rights.
3. The death penalty in the modern world is being seen as contrary to fundamental principles of religion. Not only many Christian leaders, but also many Jewish and some Muslim leaders, have joined in this view.

In so controversial an area it is always good to find common ground. Most people would agree with the proposition that no question of public policy, except peace and war, is more important than whether or not, or under what circumstances, government should be authorized by its citizens to kill people. After all, in a democracy, where the people are sovereign, when the government kills, it kills for you.

A member of the Michigan and Federal Bars, Eugene G. Wanger is the author of Michigan's constitutional prohibition of the death penalty and since 1972 has been co-chair of the Michigan Committee Against Capital Punishment. His library on the subject is perhaps the largest in America in private hands.

Reprinted from the *Michigan Bar Journal* 81/9 (September 2002). An earlier version of the article appeared in *Thomas M. Cooley Law Review*, 13, no. 3 (1996).

31. Capital Punishment in Ohio: A Brief History

Eugene G. Wanger

When Dr. Benjamin Rush of Philadelphia began the campaign to abolish the death penalty in America in the 18th century, the controversy centered mostly in Pennsylvania, New England and New York. In 1846, Michigan was the first state to abolish capital punishment for murder and lesser crimes.

Ohio was a somewhat different story. A part of the Northwest Territory, Ohio's Marietta Code of 1788 listed the five capital crimes of treason and murder; and arson, burglary and robbery, if they resulted in death. Simple arson was added to the Code in 1799. Ohio became a state in 1803 and, by 1824, the Ohio Legislature limited the death penalty to murder in the first degree.

The first Ohioan to speak out against the practice was Elisha Bates of Mt. Pleasant in 1821, but it was more than a decade before the legislature considered the subject. In 1844, a law was passed requiring the state's hangings, previously carried out by Ohio's various counties in full public view, to be performed within the walls of county jails. If this was not possible, an enclosure higher than the gallows would be built to ". . . exclude the view of persons outside."

The last half of the 1840s was marked by fierce legislative struggles to abolish Ohio's death penalty, led by House member Clement L. Vallandigham, and it was vigorously debated at the state's Constitutional Convention of 1850. These efforts failed, and interest in the abolition of the gallows languished.

After the Civil War, interest in repealing the death penalty was renewed. Many of Ohio's entertainment-loving citizens were not in agreement with the state's 1844 law that made all executions private. In 1873, a minority member of the House Judiciary Committee reported that:

> In a village in northwestern Ohio, not two years since, a private execution took place . . . although it was known to everybody that the execution would be strictly private and within the walls of one of the strongest jails in Ohio, yet not less than ten thousand people, from every direction, came pouring into the village, anxious to see something to gratify [its] morbid appetite. A strong guard of armed men had to be placed round the jail to keep back the multitude; and when the sheriff brought out the dead body, it took hours for the crowd to view the remains. And . . . at the very time the awful penalty of the law was being enforced, all kinds of amusements incident to a gala day were being indulged in by the people thus drawn together!

Twelve years later, the legislature had had enough of that frivolity and the necessarily amateur qualifications of the local hangmen that went with it. In 1885, the law required all future executions to take place at the Ohio State Penitentiary in Columbus, at midnight or as soon thereafter as practical. Although no official record remains, the best evidence is that, up to this time, Ohio had executed about 120 people.

At last regular records would be kept and the killings decreed by the judges carried out on a professional basis. Alas, that hope was not always fulfilled. During the following 22 years, prison historian H. M. Fogle documented the executions. At the prison's second hanging, Fogle noted:

> . . . [A]s one of the doctors grasped the pulse and swung the body partly around . . . [i]t was then seen that the head had been almost entirely severed from the body, and that the gurgling sound was the blood rushing from the

arteries. . . . Many of the spectators turned pale and some were made deathly sick.

Spectators made sick at an execution? This would never do, but 10 years later the same thing happened, splattering the walls with blood. Somewhat less disturbing was the unusually long time that some men took to die. This resulted when the neck was not broken and the prisoner ". . . was left to die by strangulation."

> The sounds that floated out over the awe hushed group as the dying man struggled for breath, is beyond description. The sickening sight and horrible sounds drove many of the spectators from the execution room . . . and for several minutes the terrible struggle lasted. . . . At 12:34 the quivering heart ceased to beat, just 29 minutes after the drop fell.

On a similar occasion:

> Time after time the limbs were drawn up with a convulsive motion, and then straightened out with a jerk. The whole body quivered and shook like one might with the ague; while the most hideous and sickening sounds came from the throat. This continued for eighteen minutes. . . .

In all, six of the prisoners who were hanged at the Ohio Penitentiary died like this. But we must not accuse our historian of maudlin sentimentality in reporting these details; for when some Christian women came to protest the execution of a 17-year-old (one of two juveniles hanged at the penitentiary), he forthrightly observed:

> Such sentimentality is actuated by a hyper-sensitive heart, or a diseased mind. . . . Such sentimentality is sickening, nauseating, to all right-minded people, and a stench in the nostrils of justice.

Ohio justice, indeed, seemed to be developing cast iron nostrils, for four of those hanged at the penitentiary during the period were described in the most matter-of-fact way as definitely or most likely innocent. To use Fogle's own words in the fourth case, the community believed that the executee ". . . died a comparatively innocent man."

Circumstantial evidence was most often given as the cause of these errors. Direct evidence, when available, was of course preferred. When the family of one defendant hired some high-priced attorneys to represent him, and they questioned the cause of death, the Montgomery County prosecutor had the murder victim decapitated and brought her severed head into court to show how the bullet entered her brain. Conviction and execution followed.

When Ohio switched to electrocution in 1897, it was the second state in America to do so. But problems continued and two prisoners respectively required six and five separate lengthy applications of the electrical current to kill them. I will spare you the historian's smoky details, but I cannot refrain from mentioning that the answer appeared to be that those about to be electrocuted should drink more liquids.

Here, I must pause, and remind you that I am not making any of this up. And I will pass on from the justly famous Ohio Penitentiary to more recent times. In leaving the era, however, this is what Toledo's mayor, Brand Whit-lock, later to be famous as the novelist, diplomat, historian and biographer we remember today, said in 1906 when he was reminded of the role that public opinion played in supporting Ohio's executions:

> If we are to legislate to appease the mob, there are great possibilities. . . .
> The people of one Ohio town that comes to my mind, for instance, like their
> murderers hung on a tree, and, if within the possibilities of arboriculture, they
> would like to have the tree with a horizontal limb, at convenient height. . . .
> But for our fellow citizens of another Ohio city, we would have to provide a
> rope and poles, inasmuch as the feeling of that community is expressed by
> riddling the body with bullets and then hanging it to a telegraph pole, that
> those citizens who had missed the real killing might prove themselves worthy
> by shooting at it. . . .

Six years later, public opinion expressed itself in a more formal way. Ohio's voters, by a substantial majority, rejected the proposal to abolish capital punishment submitted by the state's Constitutional Convention of 1912.

As the century advanced, executions increased. As shown by Cleveland's notorious Sam Sheppard case, there were many circulation-hungry newspaper editors that were eager to assist prosecutors, judges and jurors in sending even doubtfully guilty defendants to their reward. Another Toledo mayor, Michael V. DiSalle, later became Ohio's governor and in 1965 observed:

> The world's first recorded homicide was not punished by death. When Cain killed his brother Abel and lied about it, the Lord did not see fit to take Cain's life in return. Instead, he marked Cain as a fratricide and exiled him for life. Although we have no record of it, there must have been a contemporary debate in the suburbs of the Garden of Eden about the justice of the Divine sentence. Surely someone with the soul of a newspaper editor must have clamored for Cain's life.

Executions continued in Ohio, and by the late 1980s, Ohio had executed more persons since 1930 than all but six other states. In comparison, neighboring states Michigan and West Virginia (and America's 11 other abolition states) had executed none. Today, Ohio's grand total stands at about 467, including 19 juveniles and four women.

All this institutional activity and popular enthusiasm—like any sustained human activity—was bound to make more mistakes. A nationwide study revealed that, during the first nine decades of the 20th century, more than 400 innocent persons were known to have been convicted of capital (or potentially capital) crimes in America and 21 of them were in Ohio.

More might have been discovered, it has been suggested, if Ohio had an "open file" policy like Illinois and other states. In Illinois, where 14 innocent men have been released from death row in recent years, a closed case can be reviewed, researched and investigated. In Ohio, this type of file policy does not exist. After conviction, witnesses and evidence deemed "unimportant" by police or prosecutors are never disclosed to anyone. But there are now more than 200 persons on Ohio's death row, so Ohio's file policy avoids much needless aggravation and enhances the feeling of job security for an important segment of public service.

Questions about the justice and efficacy of Ohio's death penalty remain. James Cornelius of Canton, just before his execution for murder in Columbus in 1907, made the following statement:

> I believe in capital punishment. It is right and just, and knowing as I do that I will within a very short time go to my death in the Electric Chair, I say to you that if I had a vote tonight and could decide the whole question, I would declare that capital punishment should be continued for the good of society.

My old friend, the late Robert Domer, also of Canton, who actively opposed the death penalty, probably summarized those questions best—if very briefly—when he asked the question, "Why do we kill people, who kill people, to show that killing people is wrong?"

Bob had lived for 17 months, 26 days and several hours on Ohio's death row before he was proved innocent.

NOTE

Special thanks to Prof. Michael L. Radelet, University of Colorado, for information on the number of Ohio executions; and Prof. Victor Streib, Ohio Northern University Pettit College of Law, for information on Ohio procedure.

REFERENCES

Banner, Stuart. *The Death Penalty, an American History*, Harvard University Press, 2002.

Bowers, William J. *Executions in America*, Lexington Books, Lexington, Mass., 1974.

DiSalle, Michael V. *The Power of Life or Death*, Random House, N.Y., 1965.

Domer, Robert K. *Violence, Arbitrariness and Innocence in Capital Cases*, 13 Cooley Law Review #3, 1996.

Fogle, H. M. *The Palace of Death, or the Ohio Penitentiary Annex*, Columbus, 1908.

Halfhill, James W. *The Work of the Constitutional Convention*, Lima, 1912.

Justice Watch, Quarterly Newsletter, Winter 2002, Cincinnati, 2002.

Lewis, Orlando F. *The Development of American Prisons and Prison Customs*,
    1776–1845, Patterson Smith Reprint, Montclair, N.J., 1967.

NAACP Legal Defense and Education Fund, *Death Row U.S.A.*, Winter 2002, New
    York, N.Y., 2002.

Ohio Legislative Service Commission, *Capital Punishment*, Staff Research Report
    No. 46, Columbus, 1961.

Pillars, Isaiah. *Report in Favor of the Abolition of Capital Punishment, . . .* for the
    minority of the [House] Judiciary Committee, Columbus, 1873.

Post, Albert. "The Anti-Gallows Movement in Ohio," *The Ohio State Archaeological
    and Historical Quarterly*, January–March, 1945.

Radelet, Michael L. et al. *In Spite of Innocence*, Northeastern University Press,
    Boston, 1992.

Whitlock, Brand. *Thou Shalt Not Kill*, Ohio Abolition Society, Toledo, 1906.

Ohio Lawyer (November/December 2002).

32. Will Innocent Persons Be Executed If the Death Penalty Is Revived in Michigan?

Based on publicly available facts, the only possible answer is Yes; and execution makes a miscarriage of justice irrevocable. It usually leaves the real killer at large.

For every 8 executions in America since 1973—899 executions in all—1 other prisoner *on death row* has been found innocent. (*Death Penalty Information Center*, 2004)

Because of innocence, our neighboring state of Illinois has had to release more persons *from death row* during this period than it has executed. (*Illinois Governor George Ryan*, 11/3/03 at Michigan State University)

In 113 known cases since 1973, persons in this country in 25 states have been *sentenced to death* for crimes they did not commit. All 113 were later—most of them years later—released from death row because of evidence of their innocence. (*Death Penalty Information Center*, 2004)

In Michigan alone between 1910 and 2002, at least 15 persons are known to have been wrongly convicted of first-degree murder. Later, for most of them years later, they were proved innocent. (Radelet, et al, *In Spite of Innocence*,

1992; *New York Times* 8/26/02 p. A1) How many of them would have been executed if Michigan had had the death penalty?

In almost all of these wrongful convictions, factual innocence was established beyond doubt. Most often it was blind luck that the evidence of innocence was found.

A 1996 U.S. Department of Justice report, *Convicted by Juries, Exonerated by Science*, with a foreword by Attorney General Janet Reno, tells of 28 men who stayed imprisoned, some on death row—for a combined total of 197 years—until recently developed DNA testing proved their innocence. What about all the cases where there is no DNA material to test?

Only a small percentage of murder cases involve biological evidence that can be DNA tested. Of the 113 death row inmates exonerated in America since 1973, only 13—less than 12%—were exonerated by DNA evidence. (*Death Penalty Information Center*, 2004)

Seventeen years ago Professors Bedau & Radelet with prodigious effort uncovered 350 wrongful conviction cases occurring in America since 1900. The decade with the second highest number was the 1970s. All 350 were convicted of the capital or potentially capital crime of murder or rape. Well over half were convicted of first-degree murder. But in all 350 cases it was later discovered either that no crime had been committed (for example, seven of the murder victims turned up alive) or that the person convicted was neither physically nor legally involved in it at all. Forty percent of the 350 had been sentenced to death and 23 of them had been executed. (*Stanford Law Review*, November 1987)

How does it happen? Mostly it is false facts given to the jury. Leading the list are mistaken eyewitness identifications, perjured testimony, false confessions and "junk" science. Sometimes this is caused by carelessness and corruption in our legal system, where a small number of bad apples cause great harm. Sometimes the prosecutor in these cases had withheld evidence that the defendant was actually innocent.

No procedural or appellate safeguards can prevent these things from happening; and there is no way in a democracy to bozo-proof the justice system.

The evidence clearly indicates that there are far more of these errors than we can know. They are hard enough to find before an execution. Afterwards the prosecutor's file is usually closed tight; no court anywhere can review the facts; there is no life to be saved; the defendant's family's money—if they had any—is exhausted; and political careers are at stake if proof of innocence is found.

"The fact is that our legal system, as currently designed, strongly discourages the correction of trial errors," editorialized *The Washington Post* on November 18, 1998, "And there have been people executed whom, it is safe to say, no reasonable jury would have convicted on the evidence as it stood at the time of their executions."

Lafayette said, "I shall ask for the abolition of the punishment of death until I have the infallibility of human judgment presented to me." Has Michigan demonstrated that infallibility?

Courtesy of Michigan Committee Against Capital Punishment.

33. Documentation for MCACP "Will Innocent Persons Be Executed . . ." Issue Paper

1. WRONG MEN ON DEATH ROW, US News & World Rept. 11/9/98.
2. THE WRONGLY CONVICTED, downloaded from the Northwestern Univ. 13–15/98 Conference website ca. 11/10/98.
3. NATIONAL CONFERENCE ON WRONGFUL CONVICTIONS & THE DEATH PENALTY, 1st page of this 26 page document picked up at the above Conference.
4. CONVICTED BY JURIES, EXONERATED BY SCIENCE, 1996 Dept. Justice Research Rept., NCJ 161258, a few pp. only. You should send for this; esp. valuable for its comments by Barry Scheck & others.
5. IN SPITE OF INNOCENCE, by Radelet, Bedau & Putnam, Northeastern UP, 1992, 399 pp., is of course too big to send. It is an enlargement & continuation of
6. Bedau & Radelet's seminal MISCARRIAGES OF JUSTICE IN POTENTIALLY CAPITAL CASES, 40 Stanford LR #1, pp. 21–179 (Nov. 1997), also too big to send.
7. SURVIVING THE DEATH PENALTY, Washington Post Editorial, Wednesday, November 18, 1998.

34. Testimony of Eugene G. Wanger

Prepared for the Michigan House Committee on Regulatory Reform

Meeting on the Death Penalty Proposal

House Joint Resolution "W"

Lansing—March 9, 2004

My name is Eugene G. Wanger. Since 1972 I have been co-chairman, with Tom Downs, of the Michigan Committee Against Capital Punishment.

I urge you to oppose proposed HJR "W" which seeks to bring the evils of the death penalty back to our historic abolition state. If adopted by two-thirds of the House and Senate, the resulting campaign will waste an immense amount of time, attention, effort and money which could otherwise be used to develop effective ways to fight and prevent crime. If reported out by your committee it will divert both legislative and public attention away from productive ways of grappling with the crime problem; and I understand that many of your own House colleagues hope that you will not put this divisive issue before them.

Michigan by statute in 1846—following the lead of the American Patriot, signer of the Declaration of Independence and staunch Christian, Dr. Benjamin Rush of Philadelphia—was the first government in the English-speaking world to abolish the death penalty for murder and lesser crimes. Michigan has never restored it. Since 1964, Michigan's constitution has prohibited it.

Forty-three years ago, I authored that prohibition when I was privileged to be one of the 144 delegates elected to the Michigan Constitutional Convention. Two-thirds of those 144 delegates were Republican, most of them very conservative; yet that proposal to outlaw the death penalty passed the Convention with only 3 dissenting votes.

Today over half of the nations on earth have abolished the death penalty, either de jure or de facto.

As everyone who has followed the issue in the papers knows, this Joint Resolution is being brought up now to take political advantage of the terrible anguish and misery caused by last month's brutal murder of two fine young peace officers in Detroit. Their commander is quoted in the *Free Press* (2/19) as saying, "I'm so . . . angry, I can't see straight." I feel the same anger and join with everyone here in offering my deepest sympathy to the families of these two victims, families who are suffering a grief that I pray I will never have to bear.

But there are many persons who have borne the same anguish of having a loved one brutally murdered, and who speak out through their pain against the death penalty because they know that it can neither help them with their grief nor help society.

The recently retired Death House Chaplain of Texas, who for 15 years personally ministered to 95 men while they were being executed, writes that almost without exception the killer's execution did not bring "closure" or relief to his victim's family. All the death penalty did, he says, is inflict the same agonizing grief on the killer's innocent family, who grieve just as desperately as the family of his innocent victim. (Pickett, *Within These Walls*, St. Martin's Press, pp. xii–xiii)

Indeed what the death penalty does best is to create victims. The evidence is overwhelming that it occasionally executes the innocent, and that it causes additional murders, all for reasons which no legal safeguards can prevent.

In 113 known cases since 1973, persons in this country in 25 states have been sentenced to death for crimes they did not commit. All 113 were later—most of them years later—released from death row because of evidence of their innocence. (*Death Penalty Information Center*, 2004)

For every 8 executions in America since 1973, 1 other prisoner on death row has been found innocent. (*Death Penalty Information Center*, 2004)

Because of innocence, our neighboring state of Illinois has had to release more persons from death row during this period than it has executed. (Illinois Governor George Ryan, 11/3/03 at Michigan State University)

In Michigan alone between 1910 and 2002, at least 15 persons are known to have been wrongly convicted of first-degree murder. Later, for most of them years later, they were proved innocent. (Radelet, et al, *In Spite of Innocence*, 1992; *New York Times* 8/26/02 p. A1) How many of them would have been executed if Michigan had had the death penalty?

In almost all cases factual innocence was established beyond doubt. Usually it was blind luck that the evidence of innocence was found.

These dreadful errors are almost always caused by false facts given to the jury. Leading the list are mistaken eyewitness identification, perjured testimony, false confessions and "junk" science. Sometimes this is caused by carelessness and corruption in our legal system, where a small number of bad actors cause great harm. Sometimes the prosecutor withheld evidence that the defendant was innocent. Sometimes police abused their power. No legal safeguards can prevent these things. There is no way to bozo-proof our justice system.

Those who claim that DNA evidence will prevent these mistakes should be reminded that there is no DNA evidence in the vast majority of murder cases. Less than 12% of the 113 death row inmates who were proved innocent were exonerated by DNA evidence.

These facts clearly indicate that there are far more of these errors than we know. They are hard enough to find before an execution. Afterwards there is no court anywhere to review the facts, the prosecutor's file is usually sealed, there is no life to be saved, the defendant's family's money—if they had any—is exhausted, and important political careers are at stake if proof of innocence is found.

Moreover, capital punishment causes additional murders by the weak-minded who seek suicide by execution, by fanatics seeking martyrdom, and by those who are brutalized by what society practices instead of being guided by what it preaches.

I ask those families and co-workers who think they can only be satisfied by the execution of the killer to accept a little bit less, so that these other innocent lives can be saved.

Finally, the committee should be aware that the death penalty in America is inflicted arbitrarily and capriciously, often on the basis of poverty and race, that there is no credible evidence that it deters murder better than life without parole (which is the mandatory penalty for first degree murder in our state), that this is particularly true for police officers; and that the death penalty costs far more money than life imprisonment and severely impairs the certainty and swiftness of conviction and punishment which is society's best deterrent to crime.

In short, while the death penalty may appeal to some as being "tough on murderers," in actual practice it merely adds to the pile of bodies. I urge you to vote against this Joint Resolution and for the continuation of life without parole, and with restitution by the killer added, as a course of legislative action which will put the real needs of victims' families ahead of hollow vengeance at high public cost.

35. Testimony of Eugene G. Wanger

Prepared for the Michigan House Committee on Regulatory Reform
Second Meeting on the Death Penalty Proposal
House Joint Resolution "W" Lansing—March 16, 2004

My name is Eugene G. Wanger. I am the author of our state's constitutional prohibition of the death penalty and since 1972 have co-chaired the Michigan Committee Against Capital Punishment.

I urge you to oppose HJR "W" even as it was amended at your March 9th meeting to try provide that the only persons executed would be guilty to a "moral certainty." The amendment won't work because, in actual practice, that is the way innocent persons are being condemned to death now.

The cause in almost all these cases is false facts given to the jury, which convinces them of the innocent defendant's guilt beyond any doubt at all. This is clearly shown by what happened to the 113 innocent men released from death rows in 25 states in America since 1973. You can easily review the facts of each of these 113 cases on *Death Penalty Information Center*, website (www.deathpenaltyinfo.org, click "Innocence," click "Description of Each ...."). How this happens is set out in Profs. Radelet and Bedau's book, *In Spite of Innocence*, Northeastern University Press, 1992, and numerous other works.

The leading kind of false evidence is mistaken eyewitness identification because it happens so often and is so convincing. This has been well known to criminology students for almost 100 years. (Loftus, *Eyewitness Testimony*, Harvard University Press, 1979)

Next is perjured testimony by convincing liars. This often is caused by jailhouse snitches or accomplices eager to make a deal for a squeal with the prosecutor to reduce their own punishment. Sometimes perjured testimony is coerced by over-zealous police.

False confessions are easily manipulated out of weak-minded suspects. But they are also obtained from normal people by pressure and trickery. Both the CIA and the police have interrogation manuals showing how to do this. Of course the manuals say not to do it to the innocent. But examples of how it is done to the innocent were dramatically and accurately shown on the CBS's News television program, *Sixty Minutes,* only three Sundays ago on February 29, 2004.

Illinois Governor George Ryan, speaking at MSU last November 3rd, revealed that some Chicago police had used blowtorches, suffocation and cattle prods to get murder confessions.

The many instances of wrongful conviction by "junk" science are especially appalling because the false evidence is almost always presented by so-called "expert" witnesses called by the prosecutor or by inaccurate reports from one of America's crime laboratories. Even the FBI Crime Lab has been seriously at fault. (Kelly & Wearne, *Tainting Evidence*, The Free Press, 1998)

Sometimes a prosecutor withholds evidence of innocence known to him but not known to the defense. In all these cases it was usually blind luck that the evidence of innocence was found. All of the causes I've described are fully documented in publicly available reports and studies.

It should be emphasized that the great majority of police, prosecutors and others employed in our justice system are fine, conscientious and hard-working; and that all these problems are caused by a small minority of bad actors who do great harm.

But there is no way to bozo-proof our justice system. There's always the risk we'll have somebody who's negligent, or lazy, or incompetent, or who mistakenly believes the person he's bending the rules to convict is really guilty, or who—especially after a sensational crime—secretly agrees with the Charles

Dickens character who said, "Much better hang wrong feller than no feller." Especially when, with false evidence, moral certainty is so easy to achieve.

Moreover, executing the innocent is not the only way that the death penalty takes innocent life. It causes additional homicide by (a) the mentally ill and weak-minded who seek suicide by execution, see themselves as society's executioner or commit imitative crimes; (b) by fanatics seeking martyrdom; and (c) by those brutalized by capital punishment. As Michigan's great jurist and legal scholar, Thomas M. Cooley, said a century ago, " . . . so long as the state justifies the taking of life for crime against society, individuals will frame in their own minds excuses for taking it for offenses real or imaginary against themselves . . ."

Again I ask those murder victim's families who think they can only be satisfied by the execution of the killer to accept a little bit less, so that these other innocent lives can be saved.

My heart goes out to the families of the two fine young peace officers who were brutally murdered in Detroit last month, families who are suffering a grief I pray I will never have to bear. I share the anger caused by that crime. But the evidence fails to show that a peace officer's life is any safer from being a victim of homicide where they have the death penalty; and it sometimes makes his or her life more dangerous. (MCACP, *Would the Death Penalty for "Cop Killers" Help the Police?*, May 1999, #2)

The death penalty is not the only way to honor or show respect for the victims and it often makes the killer a celebrity, whose name is remembered long after his victim is forgotten. It's said that Timothy McVeigh, the so-called "poster boy" for the death penalty, has in fact become a "pin-up boy" for other young vicious malcontents.

Capital punishment's lengthy legal process prolongs the victims' families' grief for years and makes any restitution by the killer impossible. While no amount of money can replace the life of a loved one, murderers should be required to work in prison and the proceeds paid to their victims' families. It will be little enough, but they will be paying something back. Since 1988 the victim's "right to restitution" has been set out in Article I, Sec. 24(1) of Michigan's Constitution.

For these and other reasons, the death penalty is repugnant to many murder victims' families.

Finally, the additional dollar cost of the death penalty is exorbitant. The extra litigation and prison costs are immense. In states like Michigan, the cost studies show that they add up to millions of extra dollars a year, all of which must be paid by the state and county; and this doesn't include building the death row and execution facilities we lack. The only dollars you can save by executing an inmate is the cost of his or her food and laundry. (MCACP, *The Co$t of Capital Puni$hment,* December 1998 #3)

Experience is said to be the best teacher, perhaps because it is the costliest. In this matter, fortunately, Michigan, if it will, can benefit from others' experience. Experience which makes it clear that the restoration of capital punishment—a policy wisely rejected by Michigan for 158 years—would be a moral and financial tragedy.

It is a commonplace of history that civilization tends to resort to barbarism under stress. I ask you to help prevent that from happening in Michigan by voting against this proposed House Joint Resolution.

36. A Christian Pastor's View of the Death Penalty[1]

Statement to the Regulatory Reform Committee re: HJR W (Julian)
Rev. Lloyd M. Hall, Jr., D.D., D.Litt.
March 16, 2004

Mr. Chairman, members of the Committee, thank you for this opportunity.

So that you know where I am coming from, let me tell you that I have been in full-time Christian ministry in Congregational Churches since 1964. I have been the Senior Minister at Plymouth Congregational Church of Lansing since July of 2002. That is my background, but I speak here as an individual pastor/theologian and not as a representative of the Church.

(1) A discussion of death necessarily demands an understanding of life. Christian faith holds that life is a result of God's creation and is, for each living person, a gift from God. Whether or not any life can be forfeit—to "enlightened" medical science, to a mothers "rights," or to the state—is to force the question as to what circumstances permit us to take from someone

the gift that God has given. At the very least, the presumption of "playing God" ought to give us pause.

(2) Some will correctly observe that capital punishment is very much a part of the legalistic system developed under ancient Judaism, and therefore a part of the Christian scripture as well. Jesus specific response to a sentence of capital punishment was simply to suggest that it could only be carried out by someone who was, himself or herself, without sin John 8.7. That dictum was sufficient to effectively evacuate the sentence of death.

(3) When discussion of capital punishment rises up in the State of Michigan, it is in the context of a State with a great humanitarian experience, informed by the Judeo-Christian tradition. We seldom hear cries for the death penalty other than as punishment for having inflicted death on another human being. This is the context within which the contemporary idea of "justice" is usually raised. This concept of justice is the misguided notion that we can "balance" things.

Jesus cites the great balancing texts from Exodus and Leviticus when, in the so-called Sermon on the Mount he says, "You have heard that it was said, 'An eye for an eye and a tooth for a tooth'" Matthew 5.38. As those particular texts have been handed down to us, each in the same teaching embraces the death penalty. Jesus, however, says, "But I say to you, Do not resist an evildoer. But if anyone strikes you on the right cheek, turn the other also" Matthew 5.39. Jesus, the teacher of the Christians, rejects the notion of balancing or even retribution.

Contemporary biblical study has led to an increasing awareness that, in spite of specific texts to the contrary, the overriding biblical thrust is for Restorative Justice as opposed to Retributional Justice. Restorative Justice seeks means to set the world back on the right path; not by the extension of violence for violence, but the application of reasoned response within the context of a world that belongs to God and not to us.

(4) There is no need for any of us to be amazed that some who are the survivors of someone who was murdered feel a compulsion toward revenge. Nor is it surprising or unnatural that men and women of sound mind and good character, empathetic to the victims' families, would share that desire for revenge. But we are capable of a higher response. The Apostle Paul wrote, "Beloved, never avenge yourself, but leave room for the wrath of God; for it is written, 'Vengeance is mine, I will repay, says the Lord.'" Romans 12.19

A compassionate society, whether it be driven by the Judeo-Christian tradition or not, would care deeply about the survivors, and about the fabric of society. We would be paying more attention to helping the distraught to regain their feet and to prevent the violence in our society that energizes murder. We would not, I think, be spending our time finding ways to "get even."

Society, as reflected in its instruments of government, has a responsibility to insure safety. I have little doubt that it is, from time to time, appropriate to sentence a murderer to a lifetime in prison without the possibility of parole. But that is a far different and more moral response than to pronounce a sentence of death. Revenge is a destructive response not only to the ones upon whom we exact that revenge but upon those of us who have embraced the hatred and violence as part of who we have become. Nor can we countenance, as I am certain no one here would be so flippant as to suggest, that we ought to embrace the death penalty because it is more efficient and cheaper. Along that road would be full destruction of all of us.

Mr. Chairman, ladies and gentlemen: thank you.

Title and Distribution Courtesy of Michigan Committee Against Capital Punishment.

NOTES

1. This testimony of Dr. Hall was presented by him orally and in writing to the Regulatory Reform Committee of the Michigan House of Representatives at its hearing held March 16, 2004.

37. New York State Assembly Committees on Codes, Judiciary and Correction

Testimony of Eugene G. Wanger
Co-Chairman, Michigan Committee Against Capital Punishment
January 21, 2005

My name is Eugene G. Wanger. Since 1972 I have been Co-Chairman of the Michigan Committee Against Capital Punishment. Thank you for this opportunity to share our state's experience with you.

Michigan by statute in 1846 was the first government in the English-speaking world to abolish the death penalty for murder and lesser crimes. Michigan has never restored it. Since 1964, Michigan's constitution has prohibited it.

Forty-four years ago, I authored that prohibition when I was privileged to be one of the 144 delegates elected to the Michigan Constitutional Convention. Two-thirds of those 144 delegates were Republican, most of them very conservative; yet that proposal to outlaw the death penalty passed the Convention with only 3 dissenting votes.

I especially urge you to oppose reviving the death penalty in New York, because of the moral certainty that New York—like other states—would occasionally execute the innocent. Other persons have informed you of the more than 100 men who have been released from death rows in 25 of our states in recent years because of their innocence and how very lucky they were that it was found out.

You can easily review the facts of each of these cases on *Death Penalty Information Center* website (www.deathpenaltyinfo.org, click "Innocence," click "Description of Each . . ."). How these mistakes happen is set out in Professors Radelet and Bedau's book, *In Spite of Innocence*, Northeastern University Press, 1992, and numerous other works.

The cause in almost every case is false facts given to the jury, which convinces them of the innocent defendant's guilt.

The leading kind of false evidence is mistaken eyewitness identification because it happens so often and is so persuasive. This has been well known to criminology students for almost 100 years. (Loftus, *Eyewitness Testimony*, Harvard University Press, 1979)

Next is perjured testimony by convincing liars. This often is caused by jailhouse snitches or accomplices eager to make a deal for a squeal with the prosecutor to reduce their own punishment. Sometimes perjured testimony is coerced by over-zealous police.

False confessions are easily manipulated out of weak-minded suspects. But they are also obtained from normal people by pressure and trickery. Both the CIA and the police have interrogation manuals telling how to do this. Of course the manuals say not to do it to the innocent. But examples of how it is done to the innocent were dramatically and accurately shown on the CBS's News television program, *Sixty Minutes*, last February 29th.

The many instances of wrongful conviction by "junk" science are especially appalling because the false evidence is almost always presented by so-called "expert" witnesses called by the prosecutor, or by inaccurate reports from one of America's crime laboratories. Even the FBI Crime Lab has been seriously at fault. (Kelly & Wearne, *Tainting Evidence*, The Free Press, 1998)

Sometimes a prosecutor withholds evidence of innocence known to him but not known to the defense. But it should be emphasized that the great majority of prosecutors, police and others employed in our justice system are fine, conscientious and hard-working; and that almost all these problems are caused by a small minority of bad actors who do great harm.

The truth is that there is no way that we can bozo-proof our justice system. There will always be some who are negligent, or lazy, or incompetent, or who mistakenly believe the person they're bending the rules to convict is really guilty, or who—especially after a sensational crime—secretly agree with the Charles Dickens character who said, "Much better hang wrong feller than no feller."

Moreover, executing the innocent is not the only way that the death penalty destroys innocent life. It causes additional homicide by (a) the mentally ill and weak-minded who seek suicide by execution, see themselves as society's executioner or commit imitative crimes; (b) by fanatics seeking martyrdom; and (c) by those brutalized by the moral lesson capital punishment teaches to many . . . that killing is a proper way to handle human problems.

As America's great judge and legal scholar, Thomas M. Cooley, said a century ago, " . . . so long as the state justifies the taking of life for crime against society, individuals will frame in their own minds excuses for taking it for offenses real or imaginary against themselves . . ."

Those murder victim's families who think they can only be satisfied by the execution of the murderer should be asked to accept a little bit less, so that these other innocent lives can be saved.

The death penalty is not the only way to honor or show respect for the victims and it often makes the killer a celebrity, whose name is remembered long after his victim is forgotten. We all know about Timothy McVeigh, the so-called "poster boy" for the death penalty. How many here today can remember the name of even one of his 168 victims?

Finally, your Committees should be aware that the death penalty in America is inflicted arbitrarily and capriciously, often on the basis of poverty and race, that there is no credible evidence that it deters murder better than life without parole (which is the mandatory penalty for first degree murder in our state), that this is particularly true for police officers; and that the death penalty costs far more money than life imprisonment and severely impairs the certainty and swiftness of conviction and punishment which is society's best deterrent to crime.

For these and other reasons, over half the nations on earth—including almost all of Europe and the Western Hemisphere—have now abolished the death penalty, either de jure or de facto.

The campaign to abolish capital punishment in our country was begun in 1787 by the American Patriot, signer of the Declaration of Independence and staunch Christian, Dr. Benjamin Rush of Philadelphia. For those of you who also bring a Christian perspective to this issue, I call your attention to *A Christian Pastor's View of the Death Penalty* by Rev. Lloyd M. Hall, Jr., D.D., D.Litt., which he presented to a legislative hearing in Michigan ten months ago. I support his sentiments and have brought copies for you.

It is a commonplace of history that civilization tends to resort to barbarism under stress. I urge you to resist that tendency in New York by opposing the return of the death penalty, which is nothing but hollow vengeance at high public cost. Thank you for your kind attention.

38. A Basic Overview of the Arguments against the Death Penalty

Eugene G. Wanger

1. <u>Importance</u>. Next to peace and war, no question of public policy is more important than whether or not, or under what circumstances, government should be authorized by its citizens to kill people. In a democracy, where the people are sovereign, when the government kills it kills for you.

   Anthony G. Amsterdam, "Capital Punishment" in Bedau (1982) *infra*

2. <u>Burden of Proof</u>. If we believe that as a general rule killing is wrong, it follows that any act of killing is wrong unless it is a justifiable exception to the general rule.

   Stephen Nathanson, *An Eye For An Eye, The Immorality of Punishing by Death*, 2nd Edn (2001)

3. <u>Deterrence</u>. There is no credible evidence that it deters murder better than life imprisonment. Probably no subject in criminology has been

195

studied more. The homicide rates fail to show that you are any safer from being a victim of homicide where they have the death penalty. Recent "econometric" findings of deterrence have been discredited as junk science.

William J. Bowers et al., Legal Homicide, Death as Punishment in America (1984)

Ruth D. Peterson et al., "Is CP an Effective Deterrent for Murder?" in Acker, *infra*

James Fox et al., "Persistent Flaws in Econometric Studies of the Deterrent Effect of the DP," 23 Loyola of L.A. Law Review 29–44 (1989)

John J. Donohue et al., "Uses and Abuses of Empirical Evidence in the DP Debate," 59 Stanford Law Review 791 (2005)

Jeffrey Fagin, "Death and Deterrence Redux: Science, Law and Causal Reasoning on CP," 4 Ohio State Journal of Criminal Law 255 (Fall 2006)

Ted Goertzel, "CP and Homicide Rates: Sociological Realities and Econometric Distortions," 34 Critical Sociology 239–254 (March 2008) & see his earlier articles

4. Error. It has and will continue to execute the innocent, for reasons which no procedural or appellate safeguards can prevent. There is no greater travesty or horror that a state can inflict on a citizen than this.

Michael Radelet et al., In Spite of Innocence (1992)

U.S. House Judiciary Committee Staff Report, Innocence and the DP (1993)

Ken Armstrong et al., "The Verdict: Dishonor," Chicago Tribune, Jan. 10–14, 1999

Jim Dwyer et al., Actual Innocence ["Barry Scheck's book"] (2003)

Stanley Cohen, The Wrong Men, America's Epidemic of Wrongful Death Row Convictions (2003)

DP Information Center (DPIC), Innocence and the Crisis in the American DP (2004)

5. <u>Aggravation</u>. It causes additional homicides (a) by those who are brutalized by CP, (b) by fanatics seeking martyrdom and (c) by the mentally ill & weak-minded who see themselves as society's executioners, seek their own death by execution or commit imitative crimes.

> Frederick J. Hacker, Crusaders, Criminals, Crazies, Terror and Terrorism in Our Time (1976)
>
> William J. Bowers et al., Legal Homicide, Death as Punishment in America (1984)
>
> Kenneth Haas et al., Challenging CP, Chap. 6 (1988)
>
> Katherine van Wormer, "Those Who Seek Execution: CP as a Form of Suicide," from USA Today Magazine (March 1995) & in Mitchell, *infra*

6. <u>Fairness & Justice</u>. It (a) is inflicted arbitrarily & capriciously, (b) is inflicted discriminatorily on the basis of race & poverty and (c) is unjust even as retribution because in most of cases where it is used it is disproportionately severe.

> Charles L. Black, CP: The Inevitability of Caprice and Mistake, 2nd Edn (1981)
>
> Barry Nakell et al., The Arbitrariness of the DP (1987)
>
> Samuel R. Gross et al., Death & Discrimination (1989)
>
> David C. Baldus et al., Equal Justice and the DP (1990)
>
> U.S. General Accounting Office, DP Sentencing, Research Indicates Pattern of Racial Disparities (1990)
>
> DP Information Center, The DP in Black & White (1998)
>
> David R. Dow, Executed on a Technicality (2005)

7. <u>Dollar Cost</u>. It costs far more than life imprisonment, because of its hugely increased litigation and prison expenses. Based on the marginal or incremental (not the average) cost of incarceration, about all you can actually save by executing a prisoner is the cost of his or her food

& laundry. Even using the average cost, as most studies do, the DP still costs much more.

Margot Garey, "The Cost of Taking Life: Dollars and Sense of the DP," 18 U.C.
  Davis Law Review. 1221 (1985)
Jonathan Gradess, Organizing Around the Cost of the DP (1986)
DP Information Center, Millions Misspent, Rev Edn (1994)
Robert Bohm, Deathquest III, Chap. 6 (2007)

8. Law Enforcement. It (a) diverts money and attention away from effective ways to fight & prevent crime, it (b) seriously impairs the certainty & swiftness of conviction & punishment, which is society's best deterrent to crime and it (C) distorts the development of the criminal law.

Justice Robert Jackson, *Stein v. N.Y.*, 346 US 156 at 196 (1953)
Justice Felix Frankfurter, Of Law and Men, p. 81 (1956)
James V. Bennett, Senate Judiciary Committee Hearings on S. 1760, p. 35
  (1968)
DP Information Center, On the Front Line, Law Enforcement Views . . . (1995)

9. Protection. Society is adequately protected by life imprisonment. Convicted murderers/lifers, as a group, are the best behaved inmates in prison or on parole. Less than 1% have killed again. Doubtless better parole & prison administration would prevent most of these killings. But because it is impossible to predict who will do them, the only sure way to stop them is to execute all convicted 1st degree murderers, which would greatly increase CP's evil effects.

Hugo Adam Bedau, The DP in America, 3rd Edn (1982)
James Marquart et al., "A National Study of the Furman-Commuted Inmates:
  Assessing the Threat to Society From Capital Offenders," 23 Loyola of L.A.
  Law Review 5–28 (1989)

James R. Acker et al., America's Experiment with CP, 2nd Edn, Chap. 9 (2003)

10. <u>Victims.</u> It (a) creates additional victims, (b) makes the killer a celebrity, (c) is often repugnant to the victim's family, (d) makes any restitution by the killer impossible and (e) its lengthy legal process prolongs the victims' families' grief.

> *N.Y. Times*, "For the Survivors, the Mourning Never Ends," Mar. 2, 1989 p. 43
> Robert Renny Cushing et al., Dignity Denied (2002)
> Rachel King, Don't Kill In Our Names (2003)
> James R. Acker et al., Wounds That Do Not Bind (2006)

11. <u>Morality & Religion</u>. It violates accepted standards of morality, the sacredness of human life, the lesson of the Gospels and the prerogatives of God.

> Charles Spear, Essays on the Penalty of Death (1844)
> AFSC, The DP: The Religious Community Calls For Abolition (2000)
> Stephen Nathanson, An Eye for An Eye, The Immorality of Punishing by Death, 2nd Edn (2001)
> Gardner C. Hanks, CP and the Bible (2002)
> Hugo Adam Bedau, Death is Different (1987)
> Pope John Paul II, The Gospel of Life [Evangelium Vitae] (1995)
> U.S. Conference of Catholic Bishops, A Culture of Life and the DP (2006)
> Letters to the Editor, "Morality and the DP," *N.Y. Times*, Nov. 20, 2007 p. A22
> www.deathpenaltyreligious.org

12. <u>Botched Executions.</u> America has a long history of botched executions, producing hideous disfigurement or torture, or both. More than 40 have occurred in America since 1976. Lethal injection can produce terrifying pain.

> *N.Y. Times*, "Making Execution Humane (or Can It Be?)," Oct. 13, 1990 pp. 1, 8.

Eugene G. Wanger, "CP in Ohio: A Brief History," 16 Ohio Lawyer #6 (2002)

Deborah W. Denno, "When Legislatures Delegate Death: . . . ," 63 Ohio State Law Journal. 63–262 (2002)

Michael Radelet at DPIC's www.deathpenaltyinfo.org (December 2, 2008)

Peter Hodgkinson et al., CP, Strategies for Abolition, Chap. 6 (2004)

Adam Liptak, "States Hesitate To Lead Change On Executions," *N.Y. Times*, National Edn, Jan. 3, 2008, pp. A1, A14

Roger Hood et al, The DP, A Worldwide Perspective, 4th Edn at pp. 156–165 (2008)

13. Isolation/Association. A majority of all countries have abandoned CP, either in law or practice, including every Western industrialized nation, except the U.S. The major executing nations are led by China and Iran.

Amnesty International, When The State Kills (1989)

DPIC, International Perspectives on the DP (1999)

Roger Hood et al, The DP, A Worldwide Perspective, 4th Edn (2008)

www.ipsnews.net/new-focus/deathpenalty/index.asp

www.amnestyusa.org

14. International Human Rights. Many nations, especially those in Europe, regard the death penalty as a violation of basic human rights.

William A. Schabas, The DP As Cruel Treatment and Torture (1996)

Council of Europe, The DP Beyond Abolition (2004)

James R. Acker et al., America's Experiment with CP, 2nd Edn, Chap. 5 (2003)

Robert Bohm, Deathquest III, Chap. 3 (2007)

U.N. General Assembly DP Moratorium Resolution, December 18, 2007

TWELVE BEST DEATH PENALTY REFERENCES

Hugo Adam Bedau, The DP in America (1997) (1982) (1964)

Mark Costanzo, Just Revenge, Costs and Consequences of the DP (1997)

Hayley R. Mitchell, The Complete History of the DP (2001)

Stuart Banner, The DP, An American History (2002)

James R. Acker et al., America's Experiment with CP, 2nd Edn (2003)

Robert M. Bohm, Deathquest III, 3rd Edn (2007)

Roger Hood et al, The DP, A Worldwide Perspective, 4th Edn (2008)

www.deathpenaltyinfo.org

justice.uaa.alaska.edu/death/index.html

www.murdervictimsfamilies.org

www.deathpenalty.org

www.ncadp.org

EUGENE G. WANGER is Co-Chair, Michigan Committee Against Capital Punishment—Organized 1972 at the NCADP 2009 Annual Conference.

NOTE

Special thanks to Profs. James Acker, Hugo Bedau and Michael Radelet for helpful suggestions.

39. United States of America

STATE*	POPULATION (2013)**	TOTAL AREA (SQ. MI.)**
Alaska (1957)	735,172	665,384
Connecticut (2012)	3,596,080	5,543
Dist. of Col. (1981)	646,449	68
Hawaii (1957)	1,404,054	10,932
Illinois (2011)	12,882,135	57,914
Iowa (1965)	3,090,416	56,273
Maine (1887)	1,328,302	35,380
Maryland (2013)	5,928,814	12,406
Massachusetts (1984)	6,692,824	10,554
Michigan (1846)***	9,895,622	96,714
Minnesota (1911)	5,420,380	86,936
New Jersey (2007)	8,899,339	8,723
New Mexico (2009)	2,085,287	121,590
New York (2007)	19,651,127	54,555
North Dakota (1973)	723,393	70,698
Rhode Island (1984)	1,051,511	1,545
Vermont (1964)	626,630	9,616
West Virginia (1965)	1,854,304	24,230
Wisconsin (1853)	5,742,713	65,496
Total of Above	92,254,552	1,394,557
U.S. Total	316,128,839**	3,796,742**
% of Total	29.18%	36.73%

*Death Penalty Information Center
**World Almanac and Book of Facts (2015)
***Michigan has been without the death penalty for murder and lesser crimes longer than any other government on earth. It is the only state in the United States with a constitutional prohibition of the death penalty.

Courtesy of Michigan Committee Against Capital Punishment.

REASONS FOR REVIVING
CAPITAL PUNISHMENT IN MICHIGAN
AND WHY THEY ARE WRONG

EXECUTION OF STEPHEN G. SIMMONS, SEPTEMBER 24, 1830

BY

EUGENE G. WANGER

Appendix

Reasons for Reviving Capital Punishment in Michigan and Why They Are Wrong

Eugene G. Wanger

Lansing, Michigan
1989

PREFACE

As a long-time student of capital punishment and collector of its literature, I have been surprised to find nothing in print which is organized along the lines of attempting to identify and examine the reasons which are actually being advanced in favor of it. This paper tries to do that.

The task is not as easy as it seems; for books, pamphlets and articles supporting the death penalty are comparatively rare. Of the hundreds of items in my collection, less than twenty fit that category. This has not been by choice. I have tried hard to find them. And I think that even a partisan—perhaps especially a partisan—should always be willing to examine and reexamine the arguments of the other side.

Fortunately, I have not had to rely solely on this scanty literature, much of which was written many decades ago, to discover the reasons which are being advanced for executions today; for I have been personally exposed to those reasons over the past fifteen years and more—at many meetings and on many platforms—as an active participant in the death penalty debate.

The reader of this paper will naturally wonder if he or she is getting a fair shake, when the author has taken sides. The answer of course must be that readers simply have to take their chances. But the intelligent reader will know that it is rare to find anything worthwhile written on a complicated subject by a writer who has not seriously studied it; that it is almost impossible to study a subject seriously without forming an opinion on it; that when the subject is important that opinion is likely to be strongly held; and that in a democracy few questions are as important as whether or not, and under what circumstances, the government should be authorized by its citizens to kill people.

Some years ago a schoolteacher took her young pupils to the zoo and was embarrassed, at the rabbit enclosure, when one of her six-year-old charges asked how they could tell the little boy rabbits from the little girl rabbits. After a long and painful pause, she saw a way out of her confusion and exclaimed, "I know how we can tell them apart, children. We can vote!" I tell this story because my experience has taught me that there is something of this schoolteacher in a good many of us. We often seem to treat clear questions of fact as if they were questions of opinion; or, thinking ourselves a little more sophisticated, we sometimes conclude that when a question "has two sides to it" there is nothing really important left to say. "Yes, indeed," one might respond, "every question does have two sides: The right side and the wrong side!" But I will not push my luck so far as that. I will only say that if this paper helps to disabuse some readers of those two errors as to the question of capital punishment, and helps some readers to better organize their thinking on the subject, that will make this paper worthwhile.

The cover illustration is an early artist's drawing of the last execution ever carried out under Michigan law. It occurred September 24, 1830, in Detroit, when Michigan was still a Territory. The condemned, Stephen G. Simmons, had struck his wife in a drunken rage, whereof she died. The event and its circus-like atmosphere apparently produced a sensation and are believed to have caused many citizens to rethink their views of capital punishment.

THE REASONS BEING ADVANCED FOR CAPITAL PUNISHMENT
IN MICHIGAN

It may be surprising to see humor in connection with so serious a subject—but the story is told of a conservative Texas legislator who was asked some years ago if he would vote to abolish capital punishment. "No, sir," he replied. "The death penalty was good enough for my father and it's good enough for me."

This could not have happened in Michigan, for our state, by statute in 1846, was the first government in the English-speaking world to abolish capital punishment for murder and lesser crimes, and we have never restored it. Since 1963, our state constitution forbids it.[1]

Throughout this time, Michigan's penalty for 1st degree murder has been and is mandatory life in prison without the right to parole. Only if the Governor exercises his constitutional power of mercy to commute the sentence, is such a murderer even eligible for parole consideration.[2] Our present Governor has commuted only one.[3]

When we compare other states, we see that Michigan is one of 14 states without the death penalty, and that three others with the penalty are not using it. The remaining 34, as of March 1, 1989, had 2,186 persons on death row (including 30 juveniles) and had executed 106 since 1973. Worldwide, every Western industrialized nation has abolished capital punishment, except the United States.[4]

So with America's unique background, it is not surprising that a currently high crime rate has led many Michiganians to suggest that capital punishment is an answer.[5] While I am no friend of capital punishment, I have no animus toward those people. It seems to me that they are motivated by natural reactions of indignation and fear, and by laudable moral desires to protect the innocent and see justice done.[6] How should you and I, each of us, look at the question?

Two things I think we will all agree on. First, the main question is not is capital punishment legal; but rather, is it good?[7] Second, if we have respect for human life and believe as a general rule that deliberate killing is wrong—and I think we all believe that—then it follows that any acts of deliberate killing are wrong, unless they are justifiable exceptions to the general rule. Thus, the burden is clearly on the shoulders of those who want the death penalty, to show us why.[8]

How have they done this? Based on my experience, study and observation, I think it is fair to say that they have advanced three main arguments. These are:

1. That capital punishment saves innocent lives;
2. That it is needed for the victims; and
3. That it is required by justice.

Let us look at these three arguments and some of the facts that pertain to them.

First, if capital punishment saves innocent lives it would serve a basic purpose of government; for few functions of government are more important than protecting the innocent.

Does capital punishment do this, as its advocates claim, by deterring murder *better* than life imprisonment?[9] There is no credible scientific evidence that it does; and probably no single subject in criminology has been studied more.

If the death penalty in fact deterred murder better than life imprisonment, it should show up in the homicide rate, for with rare exceptions all homicides in America have been reported since the 1920s. However, fifty years of homicide rates show that whether one is a policeman, prison guard or other citizen one is no safer from being a victim of homicide in those states with the death penalty. Moreover, the abolition of capital punishment in a state does not cause the homicide rate there to go up, nor does the restoration of capital punishment or a higher frequency of executions in a state cause the homicide rate there to go down. And in those localities where capital punishment is carried out, there are no fewer killings near the times of well-publicized executions when any deterrent effect would be greatest. And all this was true even when the risk of being executed for murder in America was at its height. In short, there is no correlation between the ups and downs of the homicide rate, on the one hand, and the presence or absence of the death penalty on the other. It's like an automobile. If your car runs at the same speed regardless of whether your brakes are on or off, that is pretty strong evidence that your brakes are not working.[10]

Doesn't this contradict our common-sense belief that man fears death more than anything else, and therefore that capital punishment simply must be a better deterrent? Alas, a little reflection shows this belief is much overrated. Many of our fellow-citizens frequently risk or flirt with death: Mountain climbers, speeding drivers, cigarette smokers, substance abusers and those with dangerous jobs, to name a few. Have we reason to think that murderers calculate their risks more carefully than the rest of us do? Given what we know about violent criminals, the contrary seems more likely.

But even so, can't we safely assume that there are at least a <u>few</u> murderers who do weigh the risks and who would be deterred by the death penalty but would not be deterred by life imprisonment? All anyone can say is that if these gentry exist, they are such a tiny fraction of the total that they do not affect the result, or that they are exceeded by the number of additional killings that capital punishment causes.

For capital punishment causes additional killings of the innocent. These include the so-called "suicide-murder" cases, a number of them even clinically documented, of persons who wanted but feared to take their own lives and committed murder so that the state would execute them. They include the mentally unbalanced killers suffering from the "executioner syndrome," who do not identify with the executed murderer as we would hope, but rather identify with the state which does the executing.[11] They include imitative killings by the weak-minded, who are incited by the sensational publicity of capital trials. A famous example is the Michigan murder by Alfred Hotelling in the wake of the California Hickman trial in the 1920s.[12] No one knows how many murderers are indirectly caused by the moral lesson which the death penalty teaches to many: That killing is a legitimate, even desirable, solution to human problems.[13]

Is there actual evidence of this? Indeed there is, over half-a-dozen studies. The most recent by Professors Bowers and Pierce, studied all the executions in New York (which has executed more persons than any other state since 1900) which occurred from 1906 through 1963 and found that there were on average three additional homicides in each two-month period which immediately followed a month in which an execution occurred.[14]

But this brutalizing effect of capital punishment is not the most terrible way it takes innocent lives; for notwithstanding America's procedural safeguards, capital punishment occasionally executes the innocent. Professors Bedau and Radelet recently collected 350 cases of mistaken conviction occurring in America since 1900, and the decade with the second highest number was the 1970s. All 350 were convicted of the capital or potentially capital crime of murder or rape. Well over half, including fifteen in Michigan, were convicted of 1st degree murder. But in all 350 cases it was later discovered either that no crime had been committed (for example, seven of the murder victims turned up alive!) or that the person convicted of the crime was neither physically nor legally involved in it at all. In 88% of these 350 cases the state itself corrected the error; but in only about 10% did the authors find that the error was *discovered* by state officials! Usually it was a random stroke of luck that the evidence of innocence was found. But 40% of them had been sentenced to death, and 23 of them had been executed.[15]

How could these tragic mistakes happen? The two leading causes were perjured testimony and mistaken eyewitness identification, which appeal procedures can rarely—if ever—detect. Prosecutors often have to use purchased testimony of criminals to convict—a deal for a squeal.[16] When, as all too often happens, that testimony is false, the innocent are convicted and the liars seldom recant. Much has been written on the danger of sincere but mistaken eyewitness identification because it has happened so often and yet is so convincing.[17] Since it is in the nature of such errors that they are very hard to discover after conviction, and extremely hard to discover after execution, it is probable that these 350 cases only scratch the surface.[18]

Well at least, some say, if a convicted 1st degree murderer is executed, he won't kill again! Surely that must save some lives! The problem with this is that—surprising as it may seem—such repeat killings after conviction are comparatively rare and it is simply impossible to predict who will do them. Doubtless stricter parole and prison administration would prevent most of them, but the only way to be sure of stopping them all is mandatory execution for all 1st degree murderers. And that is something which, so far as I am aware, not one modern advocate of executions has proposed. Indeed, since 1976 it has been unconstitutional.[19]

Thus, both the scientific evidence and common sense indicate that capital punishment costs far more innocent lives than it saves.

Second, is capital punishment needed for the victims? Since those who say so rarely say why, I will have to suppose they mean that by executing the killer society honors or shows respect for the victim, or satisfies the needs of the victim's surviving family. But capital punishment is not the only possible way to honor the victim; and it hardly seems fitting to choose a way that will create additional victims; or that will so often make the killer a celebrity—a death house hero—through the feeding frenzy of a headline-hungry media; or that will be repugnant—as capital punishment often is—to the victim's family.[20]

While some victims' families undoubtedly want the death penalty, it is widely recognized that virtually all victims' families have two special needs which the death penalty only aggravates: The need that the legal process be completed as soon as possible, and the need for restitution.

Until the legal process is over there is no end to their mourning, and the survivors cannot leave the pain behind them and get on with their lives.[21] Yet where death is the penalty that process takes far longer and makes a speedy resolution of the case impossible. The immense publicity potential invites it and the life at stake demands it. On average, the time from arrest to execution in America is about eight years; and in some states over 13 years![22] And, incidentally, the added dollar cost of this death penalty delay is staggering.[23]

While no amount of money can replace the life of a loved one, execution makes any restitution at all by the killer impossible.[24] Georgia has executed more people since 1930 than any other state.[25] Yet three years ago a scientific poll by Georgia State University revealed that 52% of Georgians would rather have the penalty of life imprisonment, with no parole even possible for 25 years, if the murderer had to work with the proceeds going to the victim's family or a victims' compensation fund.[26] Last November, Michigan's voters overwhelmingly added a 'Crime Victims Bill of Rights' to our state constitution. Two of those rights are "the right to timely disposition of the case following arrest" and "the right to restitution."[27]

Finally, does justice require the death penalty? The only way one can discuss justice or determine what it is by referring to one or more general principles. One of these is retribution. But to make a long story short, it is widely recognized that the principle of retribution alone does not require the death penalty. It only requires that the most severe penalty we use be applied to the most serious crimes.[28] So we can be for retribution and still be against the death penalty.

Well, if retribution alone won't do it, what about the principle of equal retribution: "An eye for an eye," which has its origin at the dawn of history? The problem with this as a general principle is that for good reasons no civilized country, including America, has ever generally applied it. It would be morally repugnant to exact torture for torture, rape for rape or burning for arson; and it is no guide at all for most crimes. How would you apply it to thieves, drug users, reckless drivers, prostitutes, embezzlers or even kidnappers, to name a few? Clearly, a principle of justice which we reject for all crimes except one has no validity as a general principle at all. It becomes only an emotional excuse—a mere rationalization.

But there is a third general principle on which some execution advocates rely: That criminals should get what they deserve, and that at least some murderers deserve to die. This principle of desert is a complicated one, and it would take many pages to discuss it at length.[29] It involves two separate determinations: First, that a person is ill-deserving; and, second, what particular ill that person deserves.

Doing this in practice is extremely difficult (and some believe impossible), for it requires determining not only a person's action, but also his intentions, motives, situation, awareness and capacity to act otherwise. If we do not do this we substitute a legal abstraction for reality.

Much more important, however, is that even if we think that a person deserves to die, he should not be executed if executing him would conflict with a more important obligation. For example, while society may have an important obligation to see that murderers get what they deserve; I think all of us agree that society has an even greater obligation to protect the innocent. Thus, we can believe that murderers deserve to die, and still be against executing them. It may be frustrating, but life is filled with choices between conflicting goals all the time.[30]

I hope you think that I have addressed these three arguments for capital punishment in a fair and reasonable way. There could be other arguments for the death penalty, and I know that there are other important arguments against it.[31] If you want to read up on it, I strongly recommend three books: *An Eye for an Eye*, by Professor Nathanson; *The Death Penalty in America*, third edition, by Professor Bedau; and *Challenging Capital Punishment*, by Professors Haas and Inciardi. To learn about capital punishment is to recognize that it is more than a moral question. It requires that we also identify the factual considerations involved; for without those facts our moral values cannot be intelligently applied.

FOOTNOTES

Appending such lengthy footnotes to so short a paper calls for an explanation. The paper was written as a twenty minute speech for luncheon clubs. That is the maximum time allowed if one wants to entertain a few questions at the end. Since the subject—responsibly addressing the main arguments for CP—is a very large one, my comments had to be brief and much information, explanation and authority supporting my comments had to be left out. That material appears below.

To someone who has read the foregoing paper rather than listened to it as a speech, I can only say that there seem to me to be many more people who will read a short paper on a controversial topic than will read a long one; and express my hope that the brevity of my comments did not detract from the clarity of what I was trying to say. As to these footnotes, I solicit his forbearance with the apology of Dr. Samuel Johnson, that "It is impossible for an expositor not to write too little for some, and too much for others. He can only judge what is necessary by his own experience; and how long soever he may deliberate, will at last explain many lines which the learned will think impossible to be mistaken, and omit many for which the ignorant will want his help."

NOTES

1. *The History of DP Abolition.* Michigan's historic abolition of CP has been the subject of several scholarly articles, the most recent and complete being Judge James Lincoln's "The Everlasting Controversy: Michigan and the Death Penalty." 22 Wayne Law Review 1765–1790 (1988). Article IV, Section 46 of Michigan's Constitution, which reads "No law shall be enacted providing for the penalty of death," was adopted by the state's Republican-dominated 1961–62 Constitutional Convention with only three dissenting votes. See *State of Michigan Constitutional Convention 1961, Official Record*, pp. 595–598 and 2968 for the debate and vote. The history of earlier efforts to end that penalty in America is treated by Prof. James Davis in *"The Movement to Abolish Capital Punishment in America 1787–1861,"* 63 American Historical Review 23–46 (1957); and by Prof. Louis Filler in *"Movements to Abolish the Death Penalty in the United States,"* 284 Annals of the American Academy of Political and Social Science 124 (November 1952). Dr. Benjamin Rush, the distinguished signer of our Declaration of Independence, was the first American to write against the DP. For his remarks, together with a valuable historical essay on the American abolition movement, see Prof. Philip Mackey's *Voices Against Death*, N. Y. (1976).

2. *Michigan's Present Penalty for 1st Degree Murder.* This mandatory penalty of life without parole is prescribed by Michigan Compiled Laws, Sections 750.316, 791.234 and 791.244 (being Michigan Statutes Annotated Sections 28.548, 28.2304 and 28.2314). The Governor's power to commute the sentence derives from Article V, Section 14, of Michigan's Constitution; see the comment of the Governor's Legal Advisor in *Letters on the Penalty of Death*, Michigan Committee Against Capital Punishment, Lansing (1975).

3. *The Current Commutation Record.* The fact that Michigan's present Governor has commuted only one 1st degree murder lifer's sentence was verified by a telephone call from the author to the Michigan Parole Board at Lansing on

March 31, 1989. That Governor, the Hon. James J. Blanchard, took office in
1983.

4. *The DP in Other Jurisdictions.* The numbers of American DP states, death row
inmates and executions are from the publication *Death Row U.S.A.*, which is
up-dated and issued quarterly by the NAACP Legal Defense Fund, 99 Hudson
Street, Suite 1600, New York, N.Y. 10013. It is the only organization, public or
private, to maintain such a list. For the worldwide status of CP, see *When The
State Kills . . .* , Amnesty International, N. Y. (1989).

5. *Michigan CP Petition Drives.* Since 1973 there have been four state-wide
petition drives attempting to place on Michigan's ballot the question of
changing the state's constitutional prohibition of CP into a requirement for CP.
All four drives failed to collect sufficient signatures.

6. *Motivation.* Of course, there are sometimes politicians and others who
advocate CP for the primary purpose of gaining political power. While I have
little sympathy for persons so motivated, it seems to me that they are a very
small group.

7. *Law and Policy.* It has been surprising to me that many advocates of CP,
including a good number untrained in the law, rely strongly upon the U. S.
Supreme Court's 1976 holding in *Gregg v. Georgia*, 428 U. S. 153–241 (1976),
that CP is constitutional to support their position. If they had read the decision
with any degree of care they would know that the Justices in the *Gregg* case
majority were well aware that they were not holding the DP to be a good
policy, but only that under limited circumstances it did not violate the U.
S. Constitution. See 428 U. S. at 175 where three of the seven Justices in the
majority emphasize this at length; and especially 428 U. S. at 226 where three
other majority Justices go so far as to warn that "Imposition of the death
penalty is surely an awesome responsibility for any system of justice and those
who participate in it. Mistakes will be made and discriminations will occur
which will be difficult to explain." This distinction between *making decisions
of law* (which is the Court's proper domain) and *making decisions of policy*
(which is not), while difficult of application, is important for a number of
reasons. Not the least of these reasons is that while every citizen has a duty to
treat the Court and its legal holdings with respect, he need give to such policy

pronouncements as the Justices might make only the credence that he thinks they are worth. This is a good rule, for I think it is fair to say that few American lawyers and judges have more than a nodding acquaintance with the principles of philosophy or the tools of social science.

8. *The Burden of Proof.* Another and more worldly reason why the burden of proof rests on those who want CP is that, as shown below, the CP system costs the taxpayers so much more money. For a discussion of the burden of proof, see Prof. Hugo Bedau's *The Courts, the Constitution and Capital Punishment*, Lexington, pp. 45, 57–58 (1977).

9. *Comparative Deterrence is the Issue.* Actually most DP advocates I have encountered, either in person or in print, argue about deterrence as if our choice is between the DP and no penalty at all.

10. *DP Deterrent Studies.* There are so many studies on this subject published in scholarly journals that it would be impossible to list them here. They have been most recently cited and discussed in Prof. Michael Radelet & Margaret Vandiver's *Capital Punishment in America, An Annotated Bibliography*, N. Y. (1988); Prof. William Bailey & Ruth Peterson's *"Murder and Capital Punishment in the Evolving Context of the Post-Furman Era,"* 66 Social Forces 774–807 (1988); and Prof. Hugo Bedau's *The Death Penalty in America*, 3rd Edn., N.Y., pp. 95–185 (1982).

During the last few years some DP proponents have advanced four deterrent arguments which I think deserve comment:

First, they cite recent studies by Prof. Isaac Ehrlich and one or two of his disciples. These are a new brand of highly complicated econometric modelling studies using multiple regression analysis, and they purported to find that CP has a deterrent effect. Because this finding was contrary to all previous studies, it attracted great attention among America's scholars of statistical science. The result is that the Ehrlich finding has been thoroughly discredited, in detail and at length, by many studies specifically examining his and his disciples' work. See Prof. Stephen Nathanson's *An Eye For An Eye*, Totowa, pp. 24–26 (1987); Profs. Kenneth Haas & James Inciardi's *Challenging Capital Punishment*, Newbury Park, pp. 62–65 (1988); Prof. William Bowers's *Legal Homicide*, Boston, pp. 303–335 (1984); and Prof. Bedau's last cited work, pp.

129–132. The most prominent analysis of Ehrlich's work was by Prof. Laurence Klein of the Wharton School of the University of Pennsylvania, winner of the 1980 Nobel Prize in Economics and President of the American Economic Association, in a study commissioned by the National Academy of Sciences. After analyzing Ehrlich's many deficiencies, Klein and his two associates concluded that "it seems unthinkable to us to base decisions on the use of the death penalty on Ehrlich's findings." (Quoted from Prof. Bedau's last cited work, p. 157).

Second, they point out that during the years 1967–1972 when there was a judicial moratorium on executions in America, our country's homicide rate dramatically increased; and assert that the cessation of executions was responsible for it. They are wrong for two reasons: (1) The homicide rate increase was far exceeded by the increase in other serious crimes during the period, which were never subject to the DP, and so was part of the general crime wave then occurring. (2) Even more important is the fact that during the moratorium period the homicide rate increase was no greater in those states which had the DP than it was in the states that had abolished it. That is hardly consistent with the view that CP had been exerting a better deterrent effect than life in prison. These facts are set out in Prof. Nathanson, *op. cit.*, pp. 27–28; and Prof. Bowers, *op. cit.* pp. 103–114; and Prof. Bedau's last cited work, pp. 132–133.

Third, some of them assert that the deterrent studies, or most of them, are now at least several years old and therefore have little bearing on whether or not the DP would be a better deterrent today. While I am surprised they think basic human nature can change so quickly—indeed, all the evidence is against it—it should be noted that in fact the studies have kept up. For example, the above cited 1988 study by Profs. Bailey & Peterson reviewed the homicide data through 1984 and concluded that "They provide no indication that our national return to capital punishment since *Furman* (1972) and *Gregg* (1976) has had even a slight downward impact on the homicide problem. . . . Moreover, there is no indication here, or from any reputable past study, that the lethal problems of these serious national problems can be counteracted, or even diminished, by the threat and application of capital punishment. Importantly, this is the very conclusion reached by the Federal Bureau of Investigation, which for years has reminded Americans in its annual *Uniform Crime Reports* that murder is 'a societal problem over which law enforcement has little or no control.'" (Bailey & Peterson, *op. cit.*, p. 800)

Fourth, they argue that one cannot prove that CP does not deter murder because people who are deterred by it do not report the good news to their police departments. The inference they draw is that there are potential Ted Bundys and others in our midst, who would be deterred from killing by the DP, but would not be deterred by life imprisonment, and that we have no possible way of knowing about them. That is like saying, for example, that we have no way of knowing about traffic safety because motorists do not report in when they are saved from having accidents by traffic safety programs or devices. That, however, has never stopped us from evaluating the effectiveness of those programs and devices by studying their effect on the accident rates where they are used for a reasonable time. Why use a different standard for evaluating the DP, especially when we have fifty years of homicide rate data to work with?

11. *Killings Incited by CP.* For a description of "suicide-murder" cases mentioned in the text, see Prof. Thorsten Sellin's *The Death Penalty*, The American Law Institute, pp. 65–69 (1959); Dr. Louis West's "*Medicine and Capital Punishment,*" Hearings of the Subcommittee on Criminal Laws & Procedures of the U. S. Senate Committee on the Judiciary, 90th Cong., 2d Sess., pp. 124–129 (1968); articles by Drs. Louis West, George Solomon and Bernard Diamond in 45 *American Journal of Orthopsychiatry,* No. 4 (July 1975); and Dr. Bernard Diamond's testimony to the California Senate Committee on Governmental Efficiency, April 12, 1967, *Committee Transcript.* References to the "executioner syndrome" cases mentioned in the text are contained in Prof. Bedau's last cited work, p. 98; and Profs. Haas & Inciardi, *op. cit.*, p. 79.

Since I am sometimes asked about the desirability of CP for terrorists, it is important to note that experts on terrorism warn that the DP is actually an invitation to these fanatics seeking publicity, glamour and martyrdom. See Prof. Bedau's last cited work, p. 101; and Dr. Frederick Hacker's *Crusaders, Criminals, Crazies,* N. Y., pp. 95, 316 (1976).

12. *Imitative Killings.* The Hotelling case is described in Prof. Harrington/Brearly's

Homicide in the United States, N. C., p. 38 (1932).

13. *The Moral Lesson of CP.* As Profs. Norval Morris & Gordon Hawkins say in *The Honest Politician's Guide to Crime Control,* Chicago, p. 76 (1970), "If . . . we are to be sincere in our efforts to reduce violence, there is one type of violence that we can with complete certainty eliminate. That is the killing of criminals by the state. The question is, Will people learn to respect life better by threat or by example? And the uniform answer of history, comparative studies and experience is that man is an emulative animal." Some DP advocates respond that executions should increase respect for human life. But the maxim "practice what you preach" is believed by many, and it is difficult to convince them that killing people, who kill people, proves that killing people is wrong.

14. *Brutalizing Effect of CP.* Studies on the increases in homicide which follow executions, or are associated with them, are described in Profs. Haas & Inciardi, *op. cit.,* pp. 49–79; and Prof. Bowers, *op. cit.,* pp. 271–335.

15. *Executing the Innocent.* The evidence of these 350 cases mentioned in the text is discussed in Profs. Hugo Bedau & Michael Radelet's *"Miscarriages of Justice in Potentially Capital Cases,"* 40 Stanford Law Review 21–179 (1987). This study provoked then U. S. Attorney General Edwin Meese III to have two of his employees write a Response, which in turn produced a brief but telling Reply from Profs. Bedau & Radelet. Both appear at 41 Stanford Law Review 121–170 (1988).

16. *Perjured Testimony as a Cause.* The worst sort of perjured testimony is where the prosecutor knowingly cooperates in it. The most recent—but by no means unique—example is the case of Randall Dale Adams, convicted and sentenced to death in 1977 for killing a Dallas policeman because the prosecutor "was guilty of suppressing evidence favorable to the accused, deceiving the trial court during [the] trial, and knowingly using perjured testimony." (Quoted from the *Texas Court of Criminal Appeals, Docket No. 70,787,* unanimous Opinion of March 1, 1989, p. 26): An error which was not corrected by the Texas Courts until after another man had virtually confessed to the murder and the case had been publicized nationally in the popular movie "The Thin Blue Line." See *The New York Times'* articles of 3/2/89 p. 9; 3/7/89 p. 11; 3/21/89 pp. 1, 12; 3/23/89 p. 9; 3/24/89 pp. 1, 6; and 4/7/89 p. 9.

Even when the prosecuting authorities do not knowingly cooperate with perjury (and I assume that very few of them do), perjury is still a frequent danger because so many jail inmates will invent any story they can to make a favorable deal for themselves. According to the CBS television news program "*60 Minutes*," broadcast February 28, 1989, in the Los Angeles County Jail in California, it is a competitive business among many inmates to get themselves alone with other prisoners so that they can later falsely testify that these other prisoners have confessed; and that many persons there have been convicted by this fictitious testimony, including some for murder. This Los Angeles situation and the widespread national problem it represents is well described in the article "*No Honor Among Thieves,*" in the American Bar Association Journal, June 1989, pp. 52–56.

17. *Mistaken Eyewitness Identification as a Cause.* One of the best descriptions of this pervasive problem and how it so frequently occurs is contained in the Michigan Supreme Court's opinion in *People v. Anderson*, 389 Mich. 155 at 192–220 (1973).

18. *The Risk of Erroneous Execution.* The question naturally arises, if these terrible mistakes can happen so easily, why don't we know about more of them? Especially after there has been an execution? The three-part answer is that these errors are so difficult to discover, so difficult to correct after they have been discovered and so difficult to find out about after they have been corrected.

We are not talking here about procedural errors (although they too can produce wrongful convictions), but about errors of fact. These occur when false facts are presented to the jury, or when the jury reaches a mistaken factual conclusion about evidence before it. Such errors obviously cannot be corrected unless new evidence is found showing that the error occurred.

In his search for that new evidence the convicted but innocent defendant, in most cases, is severely handicapped by a lack of financial resources, a lack of friends able to assist him, and a lack of cooperation from those in the criminal justice system and others who would be embarrassed by proof that they or their associates had participated in a mistake. Frequently, he is also handicapped by a lack of sufficient mental ability to help direct the search from his cell.

Even if these handicaps are overcome, there simply may not be any new evidence which could be discovered to show, for example, that a witness really lied or that an eyewitness identification really was mistaken. Where the witness will not confess to his lie or recognize and admit his mistake, about the only thing that can help is new and convincing proof of an alibi or that someone else actually did the killing. And after the defendant has been executed, how likely is it that such proof will be found when the motive of saving his innocent life has vanished and the motives for concealment of those who participated in an erroneous execution are redoubled? Political careers are at stake, and sometimes serious criminal liability too, if proof of innocence is found.

And it must be emphasized that all of the foregoing has mainly to do only with those errors caused by false facts given to the jury. A much larger opportunity for error, especially in murder cases, is presented by the factual decisions the jury must make based on the legitimate—though often conflicting—evidence before it. The crime of 1st degree murder requires much more than a killing; and jury mistakes on whether or not the killer premeditated his lethal act, or honestly believed he was acting in self-defense, or was insane when he did it—all of which involve essential mental elements of the crime—can rarely if ever be proved.

Moreover, it is one thing to discover new evidence and quite another for a court to accept it as the basis for overturning a conviction. For the courts are quite naturally reluctant to reopen closed cases and grant new trials, unless the defendant can convince them that a serious miscarriage of justice was done. The law in the area is complex, and differs somewhat from state to state, but it is safe to say that the prosecutor will almost always vigorously oppose the effort and that the standards which the new evidence must meet are high. For example, a statement by a witness confessing that he lied at the trial often is not enough. After all, the courts figure, if this person says he was lying then, how can we know he's not lying now?

A recent demonstration of this is the case of James Landano, who was convicted of killing a Newark policeman. New evidence that a principal witness later admitted he had falsely identified Landano as the killer to protect a third party and new evidence that the gun used in the killing belonged to that third party was rejected as insufficient by the courts and affirmed on appeal. Subsequently, a statement by the assistant prosecutor in the case that some witnesses had been reluctant to identify Landano and had been coerced to do so was also ruled insufficient. Still later, when a witness who saw the getaway car and had identified Landano as the driver recanted his testimony, the courts held that this was not enough. This too was affirmed on appeal. Finally, after it has been discovered that the prosecutor had concealed the existence of two eyewitnesses who specifically identified the third party as the killer and one eyewitness who specifically said Landano was not the killer, the New Jersey courts, 13 years after Landano's wrongful conviction, are "letting him go grudgingly." (For details see *The New York Times,* 8/3/89, p. 13.)

Finally, as Profs. Bedau & Radelet (*op. cit.*) discovered, it is difficult to find out about these mistakes even after they have been corrected. Not one state keeps a list of such mistakes, which are so embarrassing to those in power. Unless they were the subject of a printed court decision or a book, or received truly extraordinary publicity—and in only a minority of the known cases did that happen—they are soon forgotten and become hard to find.

19. *Mandatory Execution For All 1st Degree Murderers* was held unconstitutional by the U. S. Supreme Court in *Woodson v. North Carolina,* 428 U. S. 280 (1976).

20. *Honoring the Victims?* As suggested in the text, it has long been observed that the so-called "news" value of a trial where the defendant's life is at stake, and of his subsequent execution, is far greater than when the penalty is life imprisonment; for few stories are so easy to cover, or so likely to increase circulation. For a few statements from among the hundreds of victims' families who did not want the DP for the murderer, see 8 *The Defender,* No. 2, pp. 7, 33–34 (July/August 1986), published by the New York State Defenders Association.

21. *Delayed Legal Process.* The anguish caused to victims' families by the DP's delays is well told in a *New York Times* feature article headlined "*For the Survivors, the Mourning Never Ends,*" published 3/2/89 p. 43.

22. *Average DP Times.* According to the *American Bar Association Journal,* April 1989, pp. 22–23, U. S. Chief Justice William Rehnquist reported the average time from the crime to execution is 8 years nationally, and more than 13 years

in some states. It was also reported there by the President of the ABA that serious constitutional error was found in one-third to one-half of the DP cases in federal court.

23. *The Added Dollar Cost of the DP* can best be understood by comparing (1) the actual dollars saved by not having to keep a convict in prison for life, with (2) the much greater additional expenditure required by the DP.

Dollars Saved. Surprising as it may seem to many, the only tax dollars you can be sure of saving when a convict is executed is the cost of his food, laundry and (where required) medicine. Those familiar with running large organizations will at once realize that the costs of prison staffing, programs, utilities, maintenance, and the like, will not be reduced by the departure of the tiny fraction of the inmates who are executed. As William L. Kime, Deputy Director of the Michigan Department of Corrections, wrote to me in 1973, "The variable costs which do respond to changes in population (food, clothing, laundry, etc.) now run $1.50 per day or some $550 per year. Assuming an average time served by first degree murderers to be 25 years, the cost to the state for that prison term is about $14,000." (*Letter of March 9, 1973*) The number of prisoners likely to be removed by execution can be estimated from the facts that in the 12 years since 1976, all 39 of America's DP states have executed a total of 106 persons, or 8.83 a year for the whole country; and that Texas, which has executed the most during that period (29), has executed 2.41 per year. (*Death Row U. S. A., op. cit.*, March 1, 1989) The total number of adult men and women incarcerated in state and federal prisons in America on June 30, 1988, was 604,824. (U.S. Dept. of Justice, *BJS Data Report 1988*, April 1989, p. 61)

For the same reasons it is improbable that actual prison construction expenditures will be reduced by so small a reduction of the prison population; and this for the additional reasons that prison populations (like the stock market) go down as well as up over time and that prison construction is most often determined more by political considerations than by anything else. So while a cost figure per prisoner calculated by dividing total prison expenses by the number of prisoners may be useful for other purposes, that figure greatly exceeds what you can actually save by removing a prisoner. In short, all you can actually save with any degree of certainty is the marginal or variable cost, which is far less than the average cost of incarceration.

Against this saving, we must compare the additional expenditures required by CP. These fall into two main categories: (1) Added prison costs, and (2) Added litigation costs.

Added Prison Costs. A state like Michigan, which has long been without CP, would have to build—at substantial cost—a death row and execution facilities; and an even greater ongoing cost would be incurred in running them. Richard A. McGee, head of California's corrections system, said in 1964, "The actual costs of execution, the cost of operating the super-maximum security condemned unit, the years spent by some inmates in condemned status, and a pro-rata share of top level prison official's time spent in administering the unit add up to a cost substantially greater than the cost to retain them in prison the rest of their lives." (McGee, *Federal Probation*, June 1964, p. 13) In addition, there is a lost opportunity cost to be considered, because, taken as a whole, 1st degree murderers are about the best behaved convicts in prison and many, perhaps most, perform jobs there for which free world employees might otherwise have to be hired and paid. (McGee, *op. cit.*, p. 14; Prof. Sellin, *op. cit.*, p. 18; Perry Johnson, Director of Michigan's Department of Corrections, quoted in Eugene Wanger's "*Why We Should Reject Capital Punishment*," published by the Citizens Research Council of Michigan in *Capital Punishment*, Detroit, 1978.)

Does this also hold true for those murderers who would be sentenced to death? As of March 1, 1988, 114 of Texas' 266 death row inmates were performing jobs for the prison and in prison industries there; and since the program began in July, 1986, there had been no serious violent incidents in either the living or the work areas. (Jonathan Sorensen & Prof. James Marquart, "*Working the Dead*," printed in Prof. Michael Radelet's *Facing the Death Penalty*, Philadelphia, 1989, pp. 174–175) Given the arbitrary and capricious way murderers are selected for execution (see footnote 31 below) this should not be surprising.

Added Litigation Costs. However, by far the greatest additional expense of CP is its added litigation cost. Where a life is at stake, every step in the legal process takes longer and every possible step is used. In addition, two extra steps are required in virtually all states where the DP is invoked: After conviction, an additional jury trial is held just to determine the penalty; and there is an automatic appeal of the case to the state's Supreme Court if the DP is imposed.

It is difficult for those not familiar with the legal process and its costs to visualize how terrifically expensive all this is. Some idea of the cost magnitude is shown by the U. S. Justice Department's report that in 1986 alone the taxpayers' cost of just providing defense lawyers for indigent criminal defendants nationwide was almost $1 *billion*! (*BJS Bulletin*, September 1988, p. 1) In a series of investigative articles published July 10–13, 1988, *The Miami Herald* reported, "The death penalty costs much more than life imprisonment without parole. It has cost Florida at least $57 million since 1973, according to conservative calculations based on independent sources." (*The Miami Herald*, July 10, 1988, p. 1A) During that time, Florida had executed 18 persons. A 1982 cost study of reinstating the DP in New York by the N. Y. State Defenders Association concluded, "By the time the first 40 New York death cases have been tried to verdict, over $59 million will have been expended." That is $1.4 million each and does not include the cost of appeals or prison costs. (NYSDA, *Capital Losses: The Price of the Death Penalty for New York State*, 1982, p. 26) The Kansas Legislative Research Department in 1987 estimated that the additional cost of reinstating the DP there would be $11.4 million in the first year, not including prison costs. (KLRD, *Costs of Implementing the Death Penalty—M. B. 2062*, February 11, 1987, p. 7) A 1985 California law review article on the subject concluded that, "A criminal justice system that includes the death penalty costs more than a system that chooses life imprisonment as its ultimate penalty." (Garey, "*The Cost of taking a Life: Dollars and Sense of the Death Penalty*," 18 U. C. Davis Law Review, 1221 at 1270 [1985]) As shown by these studies, the added cost of the DP is not merely the added cost of processing those who are finally executed, it includes all those cases in which the possibility of execution is involved.

24. *Restitution by the Murderer.* Convicted murderers, almost without exception, have no financial resources. The only source from which they could pay

restitution is income from working in prison. It seems much more fitting that they should be required to do this, than that the state should pay a similar amount as "compensation" to victims' families from taxpayer funds.

25. A table of *the number of executions by state* since 1930 is set out in Prof. Hugo Bedau's *The Death Penalty in America*, 3rd Edn., N. Y., pp. 56–57 (1982).

26. *Polls Favoring Alternatives to CP.* The Georgia poll discussed in the text is set out in Thomas & Hutcheson, *Georgia Residents' Attitudes Toward the Death Penalty*, Ga. St. Univ., 1986. Similar results were shown by a Florida poll reported in Cambridge Survey Research, *An Analysis of Attitudes Toward Capital Punishment in the State of Florida*, 1986; a Nebraska poll reported in Johnson & Booth, *The Nebraska Annual Social Indicators Survey*, Univ. of Nebraska, 1988; an Oklahoma poll reported in Grasnick & Bursik, *Attitudes of Oklahomans Toward the Death Penalty*, Univ. of Oklahoma, 1988; and a New York poll reported in Patrick M. Caddell Enterprises, *N. Y. Public Opinion Poll, The Death Penalty: An Executive Summary*, N.Y., 1989. Each poll showed that most respondents favored a stiff, mandatory alternative to the DP, usually one including restitution. Thus it would appear that many politicians are promoting the DP, at a time when their voters would rather have something else.

27. The so-called '*Crime Victims Bill of Rights,*' discussed in the text, was added to Michigan's Constitution as Article I, Section 24 at the general election of November 8, 1988, by a state-wide vote of 2,662,796 to 650,515.

28. *Retribution.* For discussions of what the principle of retribution requires, see Prof. Hugo Bedau's *Death is Different*, Boston (1987); and Prof. Nathanson, *op. cit.*

29. *Desert.* For discussions of the principle of desert, see Prof. Bedau's last cited work; Prof. Nathanson, *op. cit.*; Prof. Edward Wise, "*The Concept of Desert,*" 33 Wayne Law Review 1343 (1987); and Prof. Stanley Grupp (Ed.), *Theories of Punishment*, Bloomington, 1971.

30. *Conflicting Goals.* It seems infinitely better that many who are guilty should go without CP, than that one who is innocent should be deprived of his life.

31. *Additional Arguments Against CP* include (1) that in practice it is inflicted in an arbitrary or capricious and even discriminatory way, (2) that its presence in our legal system distorts the development of the criminal law, (3) that it

is contrary to the teachings of religion as set out in the Bible and (4) that it severely impairs the certainty and swiftness of conviction and punishment, which is society's best deterrent to crime.

The first argument rests mainly upon recent factual showings (1) that defendants are chosen for the DP in arbitrary and capricious ways and (2) that those who kill whites are much more likely to get it than those who kill blacks; and upon the belief that having the DP for anyone under such circumstances is wrong because the more severe a penalty is, the more important it is to inflict it fairly and equally—on *all* of those who deserve it and *only* on those who deserve it. All this is set out at length in the publications by Profs. Nathanson, Bedau, Bowers and Haas & Inciardi, cited above; and in Prof. Charles Black's *Capital Punishment: The Inevitability of Caprice and Mistake*, 2nd Edn., N.Y. (1981).

The second argument is that the DP damages the administration of justice because appellate judges sometimes distort the course of the criminal law in their sincere efforts to apply it justly to an appellant whose life is at stake. As Justice Jackson of the U. S. Supreme Court candidly admitted, "When the penalty is death, we, like State court judges, are tempted to strain the evidence and even, in close cases, the law in order to give a doubtfully condemned man another chance." (*Stein v. New York,* 346 U. S. 156 at 196 [1953]) James V. Bennett, former Director of the Federal Bureau of Prisons, bluntly testified before Congress in 1968 that, "At bottom, the retention of the death penalty has led to all sorts of controversial not to say inconsistent and erratic decisions of our courts on such things as mental responsibility for crime, use of confessions, admissibility of evidence, arrest and arraignment procedures, and so on." (*Hearings of the Subcommittee on Criminal Laws & Procedures, op. cit.,* p. 35) Such results are in the very nature of things when judges who deeply value human life are immersed in an atmosphere so incompatible with the cool, rational processes of thought that are necessary to the best application and development of the law.

Now for the third argument. So far as I am aware, nothing comprehensive has been written in recent years about Biblical teachings related to CP. However, this was one of the main points of argument in the last century and

I think perhaps one of the best 19th century treatments of it is in Marvin H. Bovee's *Reasons For Abolishing Capital Punishment*, Chicago (1878), which was earlier published under the title *Christ and the Gallows*, N. Y. (1869). See Prof. Mackey's *Voices Against Death*, *op. cit.*, for more 19th century religious views of the subject. Two excellent, but brief, recent articles are Prof. Charles Milligan's *"A Protestants View of the Death Penalty"* (reprinted in Prof. Hugo Bedau's *The Death Penalty in America*, Revised Edn. [1967] p. 175) and John H. Yoder's *"The Death Penalty: A Christian Perspective"* (reprinted in Prof. Hugo Bedau's *The Death Penalty in America*, 3rd Edn. [1982] p. 370). Recent statements against CP by the governing bodies of most major American religious denominations are set out in *Capital Punishment: What the Religious Community Says*, National Interreligious Task Force on Criminal Justice, N. Y. (n.d.).

Finally, authorities agree that speed and certainty of conviction and punishment are a much greater deterrent to crime than the severity of the punishment. Such speed is impossible where the penalty is death, as shown above. Moreover, juries have often refused to convict where the defendant's life was at stake. This has happened so often that there is a special name for it, "jury nullification." It has long plagued English and American legal history, and the *Louis Harris Poll of June 14, 1973*, disclosed that even where guilt was clear, almost one-third of the Americans surveyed were not sure they could vote to convict if the defendant would be executed. (*The Harris Survey*, Thursday, June 14, 1973) While this risk of jury nullification can be somewhat reduced by "death qualifying" the jury and by having a separate trial to determine the penalty, that risk is entirely eliminated when the maximum penalty is life imprisonment.

About the Author

A graduate of Amherst College and the University of Michigan Law School, Eugene G. Wanger has practiced law in Lansing, Michigan, for more than half a century. When the youngest delegate of his political party to the state's constitutional convention of 1961, he authored Michigan's constitutional ban of the death penalty, the only one in the United States. His collection of material on that subject, believed to have been the largest in the country in private hands, is now part of the National Death Penalty Archives at the State University of New York at Albany. He holds the Champion of Justice Award from the State Bar of Michigan.

Mr. Wanger's forensic accomplishments include being undefeated state champion in debate and oratory during high school days and president of his college's Debate Council and its chapter of Delta Sigma Rho, the national forensic honorary. He was a finalist in Michigan Law School's moot court competition and national semi-finalist in the National Moot Court Competition. As an entertainer of American troops at the close of the Korean War Mr. Wanger was made honorary member of three infantry divisions and awarded the Silver Medal by the Far East Command and the Certificate of Esteem by the Secretary of Defense. Mr. Wanger is past member of the Executive Board of the National Coalition to Abolish the Death Penalty and has authored its history. Since 1972 he has co-chaired the Michigan Committee Against Capital Punishment.

His public service also includes having been City Attorney of Lansing and chairman of the county's Board of Commissioners. In addition to numerous articles on the death penalty, Mr. Wanger's published writings include monographs on Michigan State and county government and annotated historical bibliographies on capital punishment, Michigan constitutional history, Ingham county history, the Toledo war, and the REO Motor Car Company.

Mr. Wanger and his wife, Marilyn, who is a retired Commissioner of the Michigan Court of Appeals and former Assistant Attorney General of Michigan, reside in Lansing.